GOOD ENERGY COOKBOOK

2-in-1 Guide and Cookbook to Boost Energy, Reset Metabolism, Lose Weight, and Achieve Wellness and Vitality through Tasty and Healthy Recipes Inspired by Dr. Casey Means

LAUREL PARKER

COPYRIGHT

TABLE OF CONTENT

PART 1: GUIDE

PART 2: COOKBOOK

Introduction

If you're here, you're likely looking for more than just new recipes—you're looking to feel a change in your energy, focus, and overall well-being. The Good Energy Cookbook is designed to guide you there, with more than just food; it's a comprehensive approach to vitality inspired by Dr. Casey Means' insights on metabolic health. This book will introduce you to delicious, nourishing recipes and gentle wellness practices, all crafted to bring more energy and balance into your daily life.

Throughout these pages, you'll find meals that do more than satisfy your appetite. Each recipe is designed with specific ingredients that support energy, metabolism, and vitality, making it easier for you to feel your best. From quick breakfasts to satisfying dinners, the recipes in this book prioritize both taste and function. With many meals ready in 25 minutes or less and designed for minimal cleanup, healthy eating becomes not only enjoyable but also manageable, even on your busiest days.

To support you in building this lifestyle, The Good Energy Cookbook includes valuable resources beyond the recipes. The Good Energy Meditation offers a quick, soothing practice to help you recharge, clear your mind, and manage stress throughout your day. You'll also find a structured meal plan and shopping list to simplify healthy eating, making it easy to stay on track and enjoy nourishing meals without added stress or guesswork.

In addition to food and meditation, you'll explore daily energy rituals, simple breathing techniques, and a wellness journal where you can set goals, reflect, and track your journey. These added features help make each day feel intentional, guiding you toward routines that enhance your energy naturally.

With The Good Energy Cookbook, you're about to embark on a journey that goes far beyond recipes. Open these pages to discover new flavors, experience nourishing routines, and embrace a way of living that supports your energy, balance, and wellness. Dive in, explore, and enjoy the start of a vibrant new chapter in your life.

PART 1: GUIDE
CHAPTER 1: THE BASICS OF THE GOOD ENERGY DIET

Ever wondered why some foods make you feel energized and focused, while others leave you crashing? The Good Energy Diet, inspired by Dr. Casey Means' research, is based on simple, science-backed principles to help you harness natural energy that sustains you throughout the day. This approach goes beyond simply what you eat—it's about choosing foods that work with your body's natural processes, boosting metabolism, reducing inflammation, and fueling you with lasting energy.

Whole Foods for Real, Lasting Energy
At the heart of the Good Energy Diet is a focus on whole foods, a cornerstone of Dr. Means' philosophy. Whole, unprocessed foods—like vibrant fruits, vegetables, quality proteins, and healthy fats—provide essential vitamins, minerals, and antioxidants that fuel your cells. Unlike processed foods, which cause spikes and crashes in energy, whole foods supply steady, reliable fuel.

- Dr. Means emphasizes that whole foods support stable blood sugar and cellular health, boosting energy levels by up to 30% more effectively than processed alternatives.
- Skip sugary granola bars and try a handful of almonds with fresh berries. You'll experience a steady focus rather than a sugar crash.

Balanced Macronutrients for Steady Fuel
Energy dips often come from meals heavy in one macronutrient, like carbs alone, leading to quick spikes and drops in blood sugar. Dr. Means advocates for meals balanced with proteins, fats, and carbs, which allow for gradual energy release and keep you fuller longer.

- Balanced meals help stabilize blood sugar levels, keeping your body's energy systems stable. Proteins and fats slow down the digestion of carbs, allowing your body to use energy more gradually.
- A protein-rich breakfast, like scrambled eggs with avocado and whole-grain toast, keeps energy steady through the morning, unlike a sugary muffin that can lead to a 10 a.m. crash.

Anti-Inflammatory Foods to Combat Fatigue
Inflammation is often an invisible drain on your body's energy. Chronic inflammation affects nearly 60% of adults, contributing to feelings of fatigue. Dr. Means emphasizes the role of anti-inflammatory foods—like leafy greens, fatty fish, turmeric, and ginger—in reducing this "energy drain" and helping your body operate more efficiently.

- Anti-inflammatory foods support cellular function, reduce oxidative stress, and promote clearer, more sustained energy.
- Simple Swap: Try a morning smoothie with spinach, berries, and a dash of turmeric for an inflammation-fighting, energy-boosting breakfast.

Nutrient-Dense Choices for High "Energy Return"
Dr. Means teaches that nutrient-dense foods provide a high "energy return," giving your body more energy than they take to digest and metabolize. Think of foods like leafy greens, lean proteins, nuts, and seeds, which are packed with vitamins, minerals, and antioxidants that fuel your metabolism.

- Nutrient-dense options power up cellular energy production and strengthen metabolism, allowing for more consistent, long-lasting energy.
- Simple Swap: Replace processed snacks with nutrient-dense options, like a handful of walnuts and an apple, for a quick energy boost.

Mindful Eating for Better Digestion
Eating quickly can lead to poor digestion and sluggishness. Studies show that mindful eaters absorb up to 25% more nutrients from their food, which Dr. Means highlights as a key to maximizing energy. By slowing down, savoring each bite, and tuning into your hunger cues, you'll improve digestion and gain more consistent energy.

- Mindful eating enhances digestion, supports nutrient absorption, and makes it easier to tune into your body's needs.
- Simple Tip: Take a few deep breaths before eating and focus on the flavors and textures of each bite to help your body absorb the nutrients more effectively.

Hydration with Purpose

Dehydration is one of the quickest ways to feel drained, yet it's often overlooked. Dr. Means emphasizes the importance of hydration for maintaining mental clarity, brain function, and physical endurance. Aim for water-rich foods, herbal teas, or infused waters to keep energy levels stable throughout the day.

- Staying hydrated supports digestion, nutrient transport, and cellular function, helping prevent energy slumps and mental fatigue.
- Simple Tip: Start your morning with a glass of water with a slice of lemon to hydrate and kickstart your day's energy flow.

Key Energy-Boosting Ingredients

Certain foods stand out for their unique ability to support energy production. Dr. Means highlights ingredients like leafy greens, omega-3-rich fish, nuts, seeds, and spices like ginger and turmeric as natural energizers that promote mental clarity and physical endurance.

- These foods boost cellular energy, support mental clarity, and enhance resilience to stress, all without stimulants or artificial additives.
- Simple Addition: Add chia seeds to your morning yogurt or smoothie for fiber and omega-3s, helping you feel full and focused.

Together, these principles lay a foundation for meals and habits that support natural energy throughout the day. By embracing Dr. Casey Means' teachings and incorporating these basics into your diet, you'll be equipped with practical, delicious ways to fuel your body and feel your best, every day.

THE BENEFITS OF GOOD ENERGY DIET

The Good Energy Diet isn't just about what you eat; it's a comprehensive approach to feeling energized, focused, and balanced every day. Rooted in metabolic health principles and inspired by Dr. Casey Means, this diet is designed to help your body work efficiently, supporting natural energy and resilience. Here's how adopting the Good Energy Diet can transform how you feel from the inside out.

1. Steady, Lasting Energy

Say goodbye to the rollercoaster of energy spikes and crashes. The Good Energy Diet focuses on nutrient-dense, whole foods that fuel your body gradually, providing steady, sustained energy without the sudden drops associated with refined sugars and highly processed foods. By prioritizing balanced meals with proteins, healthy fats, and slow-digesting carbs, you'll experience a stable energy flow that lasts all day.

Research shows that blood sugar stability is key to avoiding fatigue. A balanced approach keeps you feeling alert, focused, and ready to tackle whatever comes your way.

2. Enhanced Metabolism and Efficient Energy Use

The Good Energy Diet works with your metabolism, not against it. By choosing foods rich in vitamins, minerals, and antioxidants, this diet nourishes your cells, helping your body convert food into usable energy more efficiently. The result? A naturally optimized metabolism that supports weight balance, mental clarity, and physical endurance.

A well-functioning metabolism doesn't just support energy; it's essential for everything from focus and memory to physical stamina and immune health.

3. Reduced Inflammation and Better Recovery

Chronic inflammation is a common cause of fatigue, sluggishness, and other health issues. The Good Energy Diet emphasizes anti-inflammatory foods like leafy greens, fatty fish, berries, and spices such as turmeric and ginger.

These foods help lower inflammation, allowing your body to function more smoothly and use its energy for activity rather than recovery.

When your body is less focused on fighting inflammation, it can direct energy toward your daily activities, helping you feel more refreshed and vibrant.

4. Improved Focus and Mental Clarity
A diet rich in healthy fats, fiber, and omega-3s supports brain health, which is crucial for concentration, memory, and mood. By avoiding heavily processed foods and incorporating brain-boosting ingredients like avocados, nuts, and fatty fish, the Good Energy Diet promotes mental clarity and a calm, focused mindset.

Mental fog and fatigue often stem from diet. Nourishing your brain with the right nutrients helps keep you sharp, focused, and resilient under stress.

5. Better Digestive Health
Digestive discomfort can be a major drain on energy. The Good Energy Diet emphasizes whole foods high in fiber and natural enzymes, which support healthy digestion and nutrient absorption. When your body digests food easily, you're able to absorb more nutrients and use them effectively.

A healthy gut is essential for energy and overall wellness, as it plays a critical role in absorbing vitamins, minerals, and other nutrients that fuel your body.

6. Balanced Weight and Improved Physical Wellness
Unlike restrictive diets, the Good Energy Diet supports healthy weight balance through nutrient-dense, satisfying meals. By focusing on real food rather than counting calories or eliminating food groups, this diet helps you maintain a healthy weight naturally, without deprivation.

A balanced weight supports energy levels, mobility, and overall wellness. When your body feels nourished and satisfied, it's easier to enjoy meals and feel good in your daily activities.

7. Sustainable and Enjoyable Lifestyle
One of the greatest benefits of the Good Energy Diet is that it's designed to be practical, enjoyable, and sustainable. With quick, easy-to-prepare meals, minimal clean-up, and a focus on flavor, this diet is easy to incorporate into a busy lifestyle. You'll find that eating for energy doesn't feel like a chore—it becomes a natural part of your routine, bringing enjoyment and vitality to every meal.

Diets that are enjoyable are more likely to become lasting habits. The Good Energy Diet supports long-term wellness by making healthy choices simple and satisfying.

These benefits work together to create a diet that supports you—not just physically, but mentally and emotionally as well. By embracing the Good Energy Diet, you're investing in a lifestyle that brings out your best, every single day.

HEALING METABOLISM
Your metabolism is like the body's power plant: it converts what you eat into the energy that fuels every thought, every step, and every action. When it's running smoothly, you feel energized, clear-headed, and resilient. When it's out of sync, you might feel sluggish, tired, or easily drained. The Good Energy Diet emphasizes healing and supporting your metabolism to optimize how you feel each day.

Why Metabolism Matters
Metabolism goes far beyond calorie-burning; it's a series of complex reactions in every cell, producing energy needed to function. Think of it like your internal battery: a well-functioning metabolism provides a steady charge, while a sluggish metabolism can feel like using an old phone that drains too quickly!
When your metabolism is well-supported, it helps:

- Regulate energy levels throughout the day (goodbye, afternoon crashes!)
- Stabilize blood sugar, reducing cravings and irritability
- Maintain a balanced weight and support physical endurance

Studies show that around 88% of adults have metabolic dysfunction in some form. This doesn't mean you're doomed to fatigue; it means most of us could benefit from giving our metabolism a little extra TLC.

Taming Blood Sugar Spikes
Your metabolism works hardest when it has to constantly regulate blood sugar levels. Foods high in refined sugar or simple carbs cause your blood sugar to spike, triggering a surge of insulin to bring it back down. This cycle not only drains your energy but also puts stress on your metabolic system over time.

- Blood sugar instability is a major cause of "metabolic stress," which can lead to insulin resistance—a condition that affects over 30% of adults worldwide.

Focus on meals that pair carbs with protein and fat to slow down sugar absorption. For example, instead of plain toast, try avocado toast with a poached egg. It's a simple change that keeps your blood sugar—and your energy—steady.

Reducing Inflammation
Inflammation is one of the biggest culprits behind a sluggish metabolism. It forces your body to divert energy to fighting off stressors, leaving less for the functions that keep you energized and focused. Chronic inflammation also disrupts hormone regulation, further straining your metabolism.

- Inflammation has been directly linked to metabolic dysfunction, making it harder for your body to efficiently process energy.

Anti-inflammatory foods like fatty fish, turmeric, and colorful veggies are your metabolism's best friends. Try incorporating a salmon fillet with a side of roasted vegetables for a dinner that works with your body, not against it.

Supporting Mitochondria—the Powerhouses of Your Cells
If metabolism is your body's engine, mitochondria are the pistons that make it run. These tiny powerhouses in your cells are responsible for turning the food you eat into usable energy. When mitochondria are damaged—due to poor diet, stress, or toxins—your metabolism slows down.

- Healthy mitochondria are key to keeping energy levels consistent and preventing fatigue. Think of them as the spark plugs of your body's energy systems.

Foods rich in antioxidants, like berries, dark chocolate, and green tea, help protect and repair mitochondria, keeping your metabolism running smoothly.

Balancing Hormones
Your metabolism is tightly linked to your hormones, especially insulin, cortisol, and thyroid hormones. When these are out of balance, your metabolism struggles to function efficiently. Stress, poor sleep, and a diet high in refined carbs can disrupt these key players, slowing your energy production.

- Hormonal imbalances are a leading cause of metabolic dysfunction, making it harder to lose weight, maintain energy, or feel balanced.

Prioritize stress management and nutrient-rich meals to help regulate hormone levels. Adding adaptogens like ashwagandha or maca root to your diet can also support hormonal balance naturally.

Prioritizing Rest and Recovery

Your metabolism doesn't just work when you're awake—it does a lot of heavy lifting while you sleep. Deep sleep is when your body repairs metabolic pathways, balances hormones, and optimizes energy storage. Skimping on sleep or staying up late disrupts this process, leaving your metabolism overworked and underperforming.

- Studies show that just one night of poor sleep can reduce metabolic efficiency by up to 30%.

Aim for 7–9 hours of quality sleep each night, and create an evening routine that signals your body it's time to wind down. Think herbal teas, light stretching, or a short meditation.

BREATHING TECHNIQUES FOR ENERGY AND CALM

Breathing is one of the simplest yet most powerful tools for transforming your energy and calming your mind. It's something we do thousands of times a day without thinking, but when done intentionally, it can profoundly impact your physical and mental state. Dr. Casey Means emphasizes the connection between breath and metabolism, highlighting how the way we breathe can influence everything from energy production to stress levels.

Why Breathing Matters for Energy

Breathing is directly tied to your body's energy systems. Every breath brings oxygen into your lungs, which your blood carries to your cells to fuel energy production. Shallow or irregular breathing limits the oxygen supply, slowing cellular energy creation and leaving you feeling drained or foggy. On the other hand, deep, controlled breathing enhances oxygen delivery, energizing your body and clearing your mind.

Beyond energy, breathing also affects your nervous system. Rapid, shallow breaths signal your body that you're stressed, activating the "fight-or-flight" response. In contrast, slow, deep breathing activates the "rest-and-digest" system, promoting relaxation and balance. Learning to harness your breath can help you toggle between these states, giving you the energy to tackle challenges or the calm to reset and refocus.

Techniques to Energize and Relax

Energizing Breath (The 4-7-8 Technique)

This breathing pattern is designed to increase oxygen flow to your cells while calming your mind, making it perfect for an energy reset during the day.

1. Sit comfortably with your back straight, either on a chair or on the floor. Relax your shoulders and place your hands on your lap.
2. Inhale deeply through your nose for a count of 4, filling your lungs completely.
3. Hold your breath for a count of 7, allowing oxygen to fully circulate through your body.
4. Exhale slowly and fully through your mouth for a count of 8, emptying your lungs completely.
5. Repeat this cycle for 3–5 rounds, focusing on the rhythm of your breath and the sensation of relaxation.

When to Use: Midday when you're feeling drained or need to refocus your energy.

Box Breathing for Focus

Box breathing is a structured, rhythmic technique that enhances focus and helps you stay calm under pressure. It's widely used by athletes and high performers.

1. Sit upright with your feet flat on the ground or cross-legged. Place your hands on your thighs.
2. Inhale deeply through your nose for a count of 4, imagining the first side of a box being drawn.
3. Hold your breath for a count of 4, visualizing the second side of the box.
4. Exhale slowly through your nose for a count of 4, completing the third side of the box.
5. Pause your breath for a count of 4, finishing the final side of the box.
6. Repeat this cycle for 5–10 rounds, maintaining a steady pace.

When to Use: Before a big meeting, during stressful moments, or anytime you need clarity and calm.

Alternate Nostril Breathing for Calm

This ancient yogic practice, also known as Nadi Shodhana, balances your nervous system and calms your mind. It's especially effective for unwinding after a long day or managing moments of overwhelm.

1. Sit cross-legged on the floor or upright in a chair with your back straight.
2. Rest your left hand on your knee and bring your right hand to your face.
3. Use your right thumb to close your right nostril.
4. Inhale deeply through your left nostril for 4–5 counts.
5. Close your left nostril with your ring finger, release your thumb, and exhale through your right nostril for 4–5 counts.
6. Inhale through your right nostril for 4–5 counts, then close it with your thumb.
7. Release your ring finger and exhale through your left nostril for 4–5 counts.
8. This completes one cycle. Repeat for 5–10 cycles, gradually increasing as you feel more comfortable.

When to Use It: Ideal for unwinding in the evening, managing stress, or resetting during a chaotic day.

Breath of Fire for Quick Energy

This invigorating breathing technique uses rapid, rhythmic breaths to stimulate energy and boost focus. It's perfect for a morning wake-up or pre-workout boost.

1. Sit comfortably with a straight spine.
2. Take a deep inhale through your nose, then begin short, quick exhales through your nose, allowing the inhale to happen passively between each exhale.
3. Keep your breaths rhythmic, focusing on quick exhalations powered by your diaphragm.
4. Begin with 15 seconds of this rapid breathing and gradually build to 1 minute over time.
5. After completing the cycle, take a deep inhale, hold for a moment, then exhale slowly to finish.

When to Use It: Great for mornings, before a workout, or anytime you need a quick energy boost.

Breathing techniques don't require special equipment or significant time, making them an accessible tool for anyone. Start small by dedicating a few minutes in the morning, during a work break, or before bed to practice. You'll quickly notice improvements in how you manage stress, sustain energy, and regain focus.

Intentional breathing isn't just about calming down or powering up—it's about building a bridge between your body and mind. By mastering these techniques, you'll be equipped with a powerful, natural way to take control of your energy and find balance in any moment.

DAILY ENERGY RITUALS

Energy isn't something you can just wish for—it's something you cultivate, step by step, throughout your day. Daily energy rituals are small but powerful practices that help align your body and mind for sustained vitality. Inspired by Dr. Casey Means' holistic approach, these rituals are designed to work with your body's natural rhythms, giving you tools to energize, refocus, and reset as needed.

Morning: Set the Tone for the Day

Your morning sets the foundation for your energy levels. Starting your day with intention and nourishment primes your body and mind for focus and productivity.

- **Hydrate Immediately:** After hours without water, your body craves hydration. Start your morning with a tall glass of water with lemon or a pinch of sea salt to kickstart digestion and circulation.

Proper hydration improves oxygen delivery to cells, helping you feel awake and energized faster than a cup of coffee.

- **Move Your Body:** Whether it's gentle stretching, yoga, or a quick walk, movement wakes up your muscles, increases blood flow, and clears mental fog.

Try a 5-minute stretch while focusing on deep breathing to energize your body and mind.

- **Energizing Breakfast:** Choose a balanced, nutrient-dense breakfast that combines protein, healthy fats, and slow-digesting carbs.

A smoothie made with spinach, berries, Greek yogurt, and chia seeds offers sustained energy and supports metabolism.

Midday: Recharge Without Slumping

The middle of the day is when energy levels naturally dip, especially after lunch. Strategic rituals can help you avoid the dreaded slump.

- **Step Outside:** A quick walk in fresh air and natural sunlight helps reset your circadian rhythm, boosting both energy and mood.

Sunlight exposure increases serotonin, which supports alertness and focus.

- **Power Pause:** Take a 5–10 minute break to practice a breathing technique, like the 4-7-8 breath or box breathing.

Use this time to check in with your body—stretch tight muscles or simply close your eyes and breathe.

- **Smart Snacking:** If you're feeling hungry, reach for a snack that combines protein and fiber, like nuts with a handful of dried fruit or a boiled egg with avocado.

Balanced snacks stabilize blood sugar and provide steady energy.

Evening: Unwind and Restore

Winding down properly is essential for recharging your energy reserves and ensuring a restful night's sleep.

- **Create a Transition Routine:** Signal to your body that the workday is over by doing something calming, like tidying up your space, writing in a journal, or brewing a cup of herbal tea.

Choose a calming tea like chamomile or peppermint to help your body shift into relaxation mode.

- **Evening Stretch or Yoga:** Gentle movement in the evening helps release tension built up during the day and prepares your body for rest.

Stretching or restorative yoga lowers cortisol levels, promoting deeper sleep.

- **Digital Detox:** Avoid screens for at least 30 minutes before bed to reduce blue light exposure, which can interfere with your body's melatonin production.

Replace scrolling with reading, meditating, or simply reflecting on the day.

Weekend Rituals: Reset and Realign

Use the weekend as an opportunity to recharge fully and realign your energy.

- **Meal Prep with Intention:** Set aside time to plan and prepare nourishing meals for the week ahead.

Reducing midweek decision fatigue allows you to channel energy into more important tasks.

- **Nature Time:** Spend an hour or two in nature to reset your mind and body. A hike, a walk in the park, or even sitting in your backyard can do wonders for your energy levels.

Nature exposure reduces stress hormones, increases focus, and boosts overall energy.

These energy rituals don't require a major time investment or overhaul of your routine. Instead, they work as small, intentional habits that build on each other to create sustained energy throughout your day. The key is consistency—each time you hydrate, stretch, breathe, or take a mindful moment, you're supporting your body's natural ability to thrive.

By incorporating these daily rituals into your life, you'll find that energy doesn't have to be fleeting. It becomes a steady, dependable force, helping you feel your best from morning to night. The Good Energy Cookbook encourages pairing these rituals with its recipes, creating a holistic approach to a life filled with energy and balance.

HERBAL TEAS FOR QUICK CALM

When life gets hectic and your mind starts racing, a warm cup of herbal tea can work wonders to bring you back to center. Herbal teas aren't just comforting—they're packed with natural compounds that promote relaxation, reduce stress, and help restore balance to both your mind and body. Dr. Casey Means emphasizes the role of small, intentional choices, like sipping on a calming tea, to support your body's energy and resilience in times of stress.

Herbal teas provide a natural, caffeine-free way to calm your nerves without causing the jitters or energy crashes associated with other beverages. They work with your body's systems to reduce stress hormones, promote better digestion, and even improve sleep—all key components of sustaining good energy throughout your day.

Herbs like chamomile, peppermint, and lavender contain bioactive compounds such as flavonoids and terpenes that interact with your nervous system. These compounds can help reduce cortisol levels, ease tension, and promote a sense of relaxation.

Herbal Teas to Try

1. Chamomile for Relaxation

Chamomile is a classic go-to for winding down, thanks to its natural sedative properties. It contains apigenin, a compound that binds to receptors in your brain to promote calmness and improve sleep quality.

How to Enjoy: Steep 1–2 teaspoons of dried chamomile flowers in hot water for 5–7 minutes. Add a touch of honey for sweetness if desired.
When to Drink: Perfect for the evening or after a stressful event when you need to unwind.

2. Peppermint for Mental Clarity

Peppermint tea isn't just soothing—it's invigorating. Its menthol content can help relieve tension headaches, calm digestion, and promote mental clarity without the buzz of caffeine.

How to Enjoy: Use fresh or dried peppermint leaves and steep for 5–10 minutes in hot water. For an extra cooling effect, let it chill and enjoy it as an iced tea.
When to Drink: Ideal for mid-afternoon when you need a mental reset or after a heavy meal to aid digestion.

3. Lavender for Stress Relief

Lavender tea is a fragrant option for soothing anxiety and stress. Its calming aroma has been shown to reduce heart rate and blood pressure, making it a great choice for moments of overwhelm.

How to Enjoy: Brew dried lavender buds for 5 minutes in hot water. Pair with a slice of lemon or a teaspoon of honey for a refreshing twist.
When to Drink: Anytime during the day when stress levels spike, or as part of your bedtime routine.

4. Lemon Balm for Gentle Uplift

Lemon balm is known for its ability to calm nerves while boosting mood. Studies have shown that it can reduce anxiety and improve focus, making it perfect for moments when you need calm energy.

How to Enjoy: Steep fresh or dried lemon balm leaves for 5–7 minutes in hot water. Pair with a slice of ginger for added warmth.
When to Drink: Great in the morning or early afternoon for a calm yet uplifting start.

5. Ginger Tea for Comfort

Ginger tea offers a warm, spicy flavor while promoting relaxation and soothing digestion. Its natural anti-inflammatory properties can also ease muscle tension and reduce physical stress.

How to Enjoy: Simmer fresh ginger slices in water for 10 minutes, strain, and enjoy. Add a splash of lemon or honey for a comforting boost.

When to Drink: Perfect after meals or when your body feels tense.

Drinking herbal tea isn't just about the herbs—it's about the moment. Use this time to slow down, breathe deeply, and focus on the experience. Turn off distractions, hold the warm cup in your hands, and let the aroma and heat ground you in the present.

Pair your tea with a simple breathing technique, such as inhaling for 4 counts and exhaling for 6, to deepen the calming effect.

Incorporating herbal teas into your routine is an easy, enjoyable way to support your body and mind. Whether you're looking for a quick reset during a busy day or a peaceful wind-down in the evening, there's a tea for every need. With its calming properties and natural ingredients, herbal tea becomes more than a drink—it becomes a daily tool for balance and resilience.

The Good Energy Cookbook encourages you to make small, intentional choices like these throughout your day to help maintain a steady, calm energy that carries you through life's challenges.

TIPS AND TRICKS FOR MINIMAL CLEANUP

Let's face it—spending hours in the kitchen is one thing, but tackling a mountain of dishes afterward? That's the real energy drainer. Cooking should leave you feeling nourished and satisfied, not overwhelmed by cleanup. The Good Energy Diet emphasizes not just quick and delicious meals but also efficient, mess-free cooking techniques that make life easier. With a little planning and a few clever tricks, you can enjoy your meals without the hassle of excessive cleanup.

One-Pan or One-Pot Wonders

Cooking everything in a single pan or pot is a game-changer when it comes to minimizing cleanup. By combining your protein, vegetables, and seasonings in one dish, you not only save time but also preserve the flavors as they blend together beautifully.

- Sheet pan meals, like roasted salmon with asparagus and cherry tomatoes, or a hearty one-pot stew, are perfect for reducing the number of dishes.
- Line your baking sheet with parchment paper or foil to eliminate scrubbing.

Prep Smart, Clean Smart

Prepping your ingredients before cooking can save you from creating unnecessary messes during the process. Chop everything you need first, then clean as you go.

- Use a large cutting board with a built-in groove for catching juices or a separate bowl for scraps to keep your workspace tidy.
- Wash knives and utensils as soon as you're done with them to prevent buildup and make washing a breeze.

Invest in Multipurpose Tools

Using tools that can handle multiple tasks is a surefire way to reduce kitchen clutter. The fewer gadgets you use, the less you'll have to clean.

- A cast iron skillet can sear, bake, and sauté all in one. A handheld immersion blender saves you from washing a bulky countertop blender.
- Look for dishwasher-safe tools to make cleanup even easier.

Batch Cooking for Fewer Dishes

Batch cooking allows you to prepare multiple servings of a dish in one go, cutting down on the number of pots and pans you need throughout the week.

- Make a large pot of soup, stew, or grain, and store portions in airtight containers for easy reheating.
- You'll only need to clean up once, and you'll have meals ready to go, saving time and energy later.

Dishwasher-First Thinking

If you have a dishwasher, make it work smarter for you. Choose cookware, utensils, and prep tools that are dishwasher-safe so you can load up quickly and let the machine do the work.

- Avoid items like wooden spoons or cast iron pans that require handwashing unless they're absolutely necessary for the dish.

Embrace No-Cook Recipes

Sometimes, the best way to cut down on cleanup is to skip the stove entirely. No-cook recipes like salads, wraps, or overnight oats can be prepared with minimal equipment, leaving you with just a knife and bowl to wash.

- A quick energy salad with mixed greens, grilled chicken (pre-cooked), nuts, and a simple vinaigrette can be thrown together in minutes.

Clean as You Cook

The golden rule of minimal cleanup: never let the mess pile up. Wipe counters, rinse utensils, and load the dishwasher (or sink) as you go.

- Keep a damp cloth or sponge handy to tackle spills immediately, preventing them from hardening and becoming harder to clean later.

Double Duty Cookware

Choose versatile cookware that can go straight from the stove to the table. Skillets, Dutch ovens, and baking dishes that double as serving platters save you the extra step of transferring food.

- Use oven-safe pans to cook and serve in the same dish, then store leftovers directly in the pan (with a lid or wrap) to cut down on dishes.

Enlist Help

If you're cooking for family or friends, cleanup doesn't have to be a solo mission. Assign small tasks to others—someone can dry dishes, while another wipes counters.

- Sharing the load means the work gets done faster, and you can enjoy post-meal relaxation together.

Plan Meals with Cleanup in Mind

When planning your meals, think about the tools and equipment required. Opt for recipes that are simple, use fewer ingredients, and don't demand excessive steps.

- The recipes in The Good Energy Cookbook are designed with minimal cleanup in mind, so you can enjoy the process as much as the results.

Minimal cleanup doesn't mean sacrificing flavor or creativity—it means being smart about how you cook and clean. By incorporating these tips and tricks, you'll spend less time scrubbing and more time savoring your meals and the energy they bring to your day. Happy cooking, and even happier cleaning!

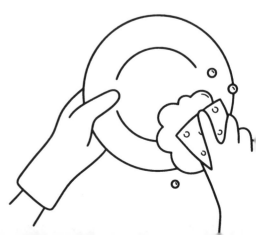

When it comes to feeling energized, what you eat can make all the difference. Some ingredients have unique properties that go beyond basic nutrition, actively supporting your body's ability to produce and sustain energy. These secret energy boosters, inspired by Dr. Casey Means' research, are your metabolism's best friends. Packed with nutrients, antioxidants, and compounds that optimize cellular function, these foods work behind the scenes to fuel your body and mind. Here are the 10 secret energy-boosting ingredients that can help you thrive:

When it comes to feeling energized, what you eat can make all the difference. Some ingredients have unique properties that go beyond basic nutrition, actively supporting your body's ability to produce and sustain energy. These secret energy boosters, inspired by Dr. Casey Means' research, are your metabolism's best friends. Packed with nutrients, antioxidants, and compounds that optimize cellular function, these foods work behind the scenes to fuel your body and mind. Here are the 10 secret energy-boosting ingredients that can help you thrive:

1. Spinach: The Leafy Green Dynamo

Spinach is rich in iron, magnesium, and B vitamins—all essential for cellular energy production. Iron helps transport oxygen to your cells, while magnesium supports the enzymes involved in energy metabolism.

- How to Use It: Blend it into a morning smoothie, sauté it with garlic as a side dish, or toss it into your salads for an effortless energy boost.

2. Chia Seeds: Tiny Powerhouses

These tiny seeds are packed with omega-3 fatty acids, fiber, and protein, providing long-lasting energy and helping to stabilize blood sugar levels. Their ability to absorb water also keeps you hydrated, a key factor in sustaining energy.

- How to Use It: Sprinkle chia seeds on yogurt, mix them into overnight oats, or make a chia pudding for a nutrient-packed snack.

3. Turmeric: The Golden Healer

Turmeric's active compound, curcumin, is a potent anti-inflammatory that reduces oxidative stress—a major cause of fatigue. Its ability to support healthy inflammation levels can give your metabolism the boost it needs to work efficiently.

- How to Use It: Add turmeric to soups, stews, or smoothies. Pair it with black pepper to enhance absorption.

4. Almonds: The Energy Snack

Almonds are loaded with healthy fats, vitamin E, and magnesium, all of which contribute to steady, long-lasting energy. Their combination of protein and fiber helps keep blood sugar stable.

- How to Use It: Snack on a handful of almonds, add them to trail mix, or use almond butter in smoothies or on toast.

5. Avocado: The Creamy Energizer

Avocados are rich in monounsaturated fats, which provide a slow-burning source of fuel. They're also packed with potassium, a key electrolyte that supports muscle function and energy levels.

- How to Use It: Spread avocado on toast, slice it into salads, or blend it into a creamy dressing or smoothie.

6. Wild Salmon: The Omega-3 Superstar

Wild salmon is an excellent source of omega-3 fatty acids, which reduce inflammation and support brain function. Its high protein content also aids in muscle repair and energy production.

- How to Use It: Grill or bake salmon for dinner, flake it into a salad, or add it to an omelet for a hearty breakfast.

7. Quinoa: The Ancient Grain of Energy

Quinoa is a complete protein, containing all nine essential amino acids, and is a great source of complex carbohydrates. Its high fiber content ensures a gradual energy release, keeping you powered for longer.

- How to Use It: Use quinoa as a base for grain bowls, mix it into soups, or enjoy it as a side dish with roasted vegetables.

8. Blueberries: Nature's Energy Bites

Blueberries are antioxidant-rich, protecting your cells from oxidative damage that can lead to fatigue. They're also high in natural sugars and fiber, providing a quick but steady energy boost.

- How to Use It: Add blueberries to oatmeal, smoothies, or yogurt, or enjoy them as a simple snack on their own.

9. Eggs: The Protein Powerhouse

Eggs are a complete protein source and rich in B vitamins, which are crucial for converting food into usable energy. They're also packed with choline, a nutrient that supports brain health.

- How to Use It: Enjoy eggs boiled, scrambled, or as part of a frittata for a versatile, energy-boosting meal.

10. Dark Chocolate: The Sweet Energizer

Dark chocolate (70% cocoa or higher) contains theobromine, a compound that provides a gentle energy lift without the jitters of caffeine. It's also rich in antioxidants and magnesium, both of which support energy production.

- How to Use It: Eat a square of dark chocolate as a treat, melt it into oatmeal, or use it as a topping for fruit.

EXERCISES FOR ENERGY ACTIVATION

Sometimes, the quickest way to boost your energy isn't through food or rest—it's by moving your body. Physical activity doesn't have to mean a full workout; even a few minutes of intentional movement can activate your energy systems, improve circulation, and clear mental fog. Dr. Casey Means highlights the importance of daily movement in promoting metabolic health and sustained energy, emphasizing that small bursts of exercise can make a big difference.

Here's how to activate your energy with simple, effective exercises that can be done almost anywhere.

Dynamic Stretching for a Quick Wake-Up

Dynamic stretches involve controlled movements that warm up your muscles and increase blood flow. These are perfect for jumpstarting your energy in the morning or after sitting for extended periods.

- **Arm Circles:** Extend your arms out to the sides and make small, controlled circles, gradually increasing the size. Do 15–20 seconds in each direction.
- **Leg Swings:** Hold onto a stable surface and swing one leg forward and backward, keeping it straight. Do 10 swings per leg.
- **Cat-Cow Stretch:** On all fours, alternate between arching your back (Cow) and rounding it (Cat). Repeat for 10 breaths.

Dynamic stretches increase circulation, warm up your muscles, and loosen stiff joints, preparing your body for activity and boosting energy levels.

Power Walks for Circulation and Clarity

A brisk 5–10 minute walk can do wonders for your energy and mental focus. Walking activates your muscles, gets your heart rate up, and increases oxygen flow to your brain.

1. Find a clear space indoors or outdoors and walk at a steady pace.
2. Swing your arms naturally and focus on your breathing, inhaling deeply and exhaling fully.

Studies show that short bursts of walking can reduce fatigue by increasing endorphins and improving circulation. It's also an easy way to refresh your mind during a midday slump.

High Knees for a Quick Energy Boost

High knees are a simple cardio exercise that gets your blood pumping and activates your core and leg muscles.

1. Stand tall with your feet hip-width apart.
2. Raise one knee toward your chest, then quickly switch to the other knee.
3. Pump your arms as you move, maintaining a quick but controlled rhythm.
4. Continue for 30 seconds to 1 minute.

High knees elevate your heart rate and increase oxygen flow, giving you an instant burst of energy.

Chair Squats for Strength and Activation

Chair squats engage your legs, glutes, and core, activating large muscle groups that boost your metabolism and energy levels.

1. Stand in front of a sturdy chair with your feet shoulder-width apart.
2. Lower your body as if you're about to sit down, keeping your back straight and your knees aligned over your toes.
3. Hover just above the chair for a moment, then stand back up.
4. Repeat 10–12 times.

Squats engage multiple muscles, promoting better circulation and activating energy reserves without requiring extensive time or space.

Standing Side Stretches for Mental Refresh

Side stretches relieve tension in your upper body and improve spinal mobility, helping you feel more relaxed and focused.

1. Stand tall with your feet hip-width apart.
2. Reach one arm overhead and lean gently to the opposite side, feeling a stretch along your side.
3. Hold for 15 seconds, then switch sides.
4. Repeat 2–3 times per side.
5. Stretching your sides improves circulation to the torso and relieves tension caused by sitting or stress, helping you feel more energized and mobile.

Plank Holds for Core Activation

Planks are a full-body exercise that strengthens your core, arms, and shoulders while improving posture and endurance.

1. Get into a push-up position, with your hands directly under your shoulders and your body forming a straight line from head to heels.
2. Engage your core and hold the position for 20–30 seconds, gradually increasing your time as you build strength.
3. If needed, modify by dropping to your knees while keeping your back straight.

Planks activate major muscle groups and stabilize your core, helping improve your overall strength and energy efficiency.

Seated Twists for Relaxation and Energy

Seated twists are great for re-energizing your body after long periods of sitting. They stretch your spine and improve circulation to your internal organs, leaving you refreshed.

1. Sit on a chair with your feet flat on the ground.
2. Place your right hand on the back of the chair and your left hand on your right knee.
3. Gently twist your torso to the right, holding for 10–15 seconds.
4. Return to center and repeat on the other side.
5. Perform 2–3 repetitions on each side.

Twisting movements stimulate circulation and relieve tension in the lower back, promoting a relaxed yet energized state.

Breath-Synchronized Movements for Calm Energy

Combining movement with intentional breathing can help you feel both calm and energized at once. Yoga-inspired movements like sun salutations or flow sequences are perfect for this.

1. Start standing, inhale as you raise your arms overhead, and exhale as you fold forward.
2. Inhale to lift halfway up with a flat back, and exhale to fold again.
3. Repeat the sequence for 2–3 minutes, moving with your breath.

This rhythmic movement promotes relaxation while increasing blood flow and oxygen delivery to your cells.

These exercises don't require a gym, special equipment, or a large time commitment—just a few minutes of intentional movement can be enough to activate your energy. Whether it's starting your day with dynamic stretches, taking a midday walk, or ending with a calming flow, these practices help reset your energy whenever you need it.

MINDFUL EATING AND PREPARATION

In a world where meals are often rushed or multitasked, mindful eating offers a refreshing approach that brings intention, awareness, and satisfaction to the way we nourish our bodies. It's about more than just slowing down; it's about truly connecting with your food, appreciating its flavors, and understanding how it fuels your body.

Mindful eating isn't just a trend—it's backed by science. Studies show that when you eat mindfully, you're more likely to:

- **Absorb nutrients efficiently**, supporting steady energy levels.
- **Avoid overeating**, as you're better tuned to your body's hunger and fullness cues.
- **Reduce stress,** as the act of eating with awareness engages the body's relaxation response.

By being present during meals, you create a space for your mind and body to align, transforming a basic necessity into an act of self-care.

Create a Calm Eating Environment
Before you eat, take a moment to set the stage. Eliminate distractions like phones, TVs, or laptops, and focus solely on the act of eating. This helps you tune into your body and the experience of your meal.
- Light a candle, play soft music, or simply take a few deep breaths before beginning your meal. These small actions can help signal to your mind and body that it's time to slow down and enjoy.

Engage Your Senses
Take a moment to observe your meal. Look at the colors, inhale the aromas, and notice the textures. When you take your first bite, pay attention to the flavors and how they change as you chew.
- Engaging your senses enhances satisfaction, making each meal more enjoyable. This connection also helps you appreciate your food, promoting gratitude and mindfulness.

Chew Slowly and Thoroughly
Chewing your food thoroughly allows your digestive system to work more efficiently, breaking down
- Aim to chew each bite at least 15–20 times, or until the food's texture becomes smooth. This gives your body time to recognize fullness and prevents overeating.

Listen to Your Body
Mindful eating involves tuning in to your body's signals of hunger and satiety. Eat when you're truly hungry, and stop when you feel comfortably full, rather than when your plate is empty.
- Halfway through your meal, pause and ask yourself, "Am I still hungry, or am I eating out of habit?" This simple check-in can help you stay aligned with your body's needs.

Mindful Preparation: Starting with Intention
Mindfulness doesn't begin at the table—it starts in the kitchen. Preparing your meals with care and intention allows you to connect with the process of nourishing yourself, making the act of cooking feel more meaningful.

Choose Quality Ingredients
Mindful preparation begins with selecting fresh, nutrient-rich ingredients. Knowing where your food comes from and choosing high-quality options helps you feel more connected to what you're eating.
- Shop with a list and take a moment to appreciate the colors, textures, and scents of your ingredients as you choose them.

Simplify the Process
Mindful cooking doesn't mean spending hours in the kitchen. Instead, it's about focusing on the experience rather than rushing through it. Enjoy the sound of chopping vegetables, the smell of spices, and the sight of your meal coming together.
- Choose recipes that are simple yet flavorful, allowing you to focus on the act of cooking without feeling overwhelmed. Many recipes in The Good Energy Cookbook are designed to make preparation easy and enjoyable.

Cook with Gratitude
As you prepare your meal, take a moment to reflect on the journey your ingredients took to reach your plate. Gratitude for the process fosters a deeper connection to your food and enhances the mindfulness of the experience.

Try saying a silent "thank you" for your meal before you start eating—it's a small ritual that can shift your mindset to one of appreciation.

Mindful eating and preparation go hand in hand with the principles of the Good Energy Diet. By paying attention to what you're eating, how it's prepared, and how it makes you feel, you're giving your body the best chance to absorb nutrients, support metabolism, and sustain steady energy.

When you combine nutrient-dense meals with mindful practices, you're not just feeding your body—you're nourishing your mind and spirit. Mindful eating turns every meal into an opportunity for self-care, ensuring that food is both a source of energy and joy.

WELLNESS JOURNAL

A wellness journal isn't just a notebook; it's your personal guide to understanding your body, tracking your progress, and cultivating mindfulness in your daily life. It's where you can reflect on what's working, identify areas for improvement, and celebrate small victories. In the Good Energy Diet, a wellness journal becomes an essential tool for sustaining energy, balance, and overall well-being.

Life moves fast, and it's easy to lose track of how your habits, meals, and routines affect your energy and mood. A wellness journal helps you slow down and tune into your body's signals. Research shows that self-tracking can improve consistency and accountability, making it more likely that you'll stick to positive changes over time.

- **Clarity**: Writing things down helps you identify patterns in your energy, sleep, or digestion, making it easier to spot triggers or habits that need adjustment.
- **Motivation**: Seeing your progress—even small steps—can keep you inspired and committed to your wellness journey.
- **Mindfulness**: Reflecting in a journal encourages you to stay present, turning everyday choices into intentional actions.

Your wellness journal is as unique as you are, but here are some key elements to get you started:

Daily Energy Levels
Track how you feel throughout the day. Are you energized in the morning but crashing mid-afternoon? Recording this can help you align your meals, rituals, and routines to support steady energy.
Prompt: "What time of day do I feel my best? When do I feel low energy?"
Example: "Felt focused from 9 a.m.–11 a.m. after a balanced breakfast. Energy dipped at 3 p.m.—consider adding a protein-based snack."

Meal and Snack Logs
Record what you eat and how it makes you feel. This can help you notice how certain foods impact your energy, digestion, or mood.
Prompt: "What did I eat today, and how did it make me feel afterward?"
Example: "Lunch: Grilled chicken salad. Felt energized and light. Dinner: Pasta with heavy cream—felt bloated and tired."

Hydration Tracking
Staying hydrated is crucial for sustained energy, yet it's easy to forget. Keep a record of your water intake and how it correlates with your energy levels.
Prompt: "Did I drink enough water today? How did I feel when I stayed hydrated?"
Example: "Drank 8 glasses today—felt more focused. Only had 3 yesterday—felt sluggish."

Sleep Quality
Sleep is a cornerstone of energy and metabolic health. Use your journal to track not just how long you sleep, but also how restful it feels.
Prompt: "How did I sleep last night, and how do I feel this morning?"
Example: "7 hours of deep sleep—woke up refreshed. 5 hours with interruptions—felt groggy and irritable."

Gratitude Practice
A gratitude section can help you focus on the positive and stay motivated. Writing down even one thing you're grateful for each day shifts your mindset to one of abundance and appreciation.
Prompt: "What am I grateful for today?"
Example: "Grateful for a sunny walk during lunch and a delicious smoothie to start my day."

Consistency is key to getting the most out of your wellness journal. Dedicate just 5–10 minutes each day—either in the morning to set intentions or in the evening to reflect. Keep your journal in a place where you'll see it often, like your bedside table or kitchen counter, and make it part of your routine.

Incorporating a wellness journal into the Good Energy Diet helps you take an active role in your health journey. It bridges the gap between what you eat, how you live, and how you feel, empowering you to make adjustments that work best for your unique body. The journal becomes your accountability partner, your space for reflection, and your roadmap to sustained energy and balance.

GOOD ENERGY MEDITATION

Before you begin, find a comfortable place where you won't be disturbed for a few minutes. You can sit on a chair, lie down, or rest on a cushion—whatever feels most natural and supportive for you. If you'd like, turn on some soft meditation music from YouTube—look for tracks with frequencies around 432 Hz or 528 Hz, known for their calming, energy-balancing properties.

Now, gently close your eyes and let your hands rest comfortably on your lap or by your sides. Take a slow, deep breath in through your nose... (pause for 4 seconds) ...and exhale slowly through your mouth. (pause for 4 seconds) Feel your body beginning to relax.

With each breath, allow yourself to arrive fully in this moment. Let go of what came before and what's waiting later. This time is just for you. (pause)

Take another deep breath in. Imagine drawing in fresh, vibrant energy with your inhale—a warm, golden light filling your lungs. (pause) As you exhale, picture releasing all the tension, fatigue, or stress you've been carrying. Imagine it leaving your body like a soft grey mist, dissolving with the breath. (pause)

Now, bring your attention to the top of your head. Picture that golden light gently resting there, like the first rays of morning sunlight touching your skin. With your next breath, let that light begin to move downward—slowly, softly—warming and relaxing every muscle it touches.

- Feel it sweep across your forehead, smoothing away any lines of tension. (pause for 5 seconds)
- Let it travel to your eyes, relaxing the space around them. Notice how your jaw softens as the light moves through your cheeks and mouth. (pause)
- Feel your neck loosen as the golden energy moves into your shoulders, melting away any tightness. Imagine the tension flowing out with each exhale. (pause for 5 seconds)

With every breath, the light moves deeper—down your arms, all the way to your fingertips. Your arms feel heavy, warm, and relaxed. (pause for 5 seconds)
Now, bring your focus to your chest. Feel the light gather around your heart, glowing brighter with every inhale. Let this light fill you with warmth, clarity, and a deep sense of calm. (pause for 10 seconds) Visualize this energy radiating outward, filling your entire chest with positivity and balance.

As the golden light moves into your stomach, feel your breath deepen naturally. Let your belly rise and fall, soothing your digestive system and relaxing your core. (pause for 5 seconds)

With each breath, allow the light to flow through your hips, legs, and knees—softening any stiffness as it travels. (pause) Let it move all the way down to your feet, grounding you. Feel a sense of connection with the earth beneath you—steady, calm, and strong. (pause for 5 seconds)

Now, imagine that golden light filling your entire body—head to toe—a warm glow of pure energy, confidence, and balance. Stay with this feeling for a few deep breaths. Inhale... "I am energized." (pause) Exhale... "I release what no longer serves me." (pause)

Allow yourself to sit with this feeling of calm, steady power. If any thoughts arise, let them drift by without judgment, bringing your focus gently back to your breath and that golden light. (pause for 10 seconds)

When you're ready, begin to bring awareness back to your surroundings. Gently wiggle your fingers and toes, feeling your energy refreshed and your mind clear.

Take a final, deep breath in—drawing in gratitude for this moment—and exhale slowly. Open your eyes when it feels natural, and carry this renewed energy with you into the rest of your day. You are calm, grounded, and ready to thrive.

Spinach & Feta Egg Skillet

 Prep Time: 5 minutes *Cook Time: 10 minutes* *Total Time: 15 minutes*
 Yield: 2 servings

Ingredients

- 1 cup fresh spinach
- 2 large eggs
- ¼ cup crumbled feta cheese
- Salt and pepper, to taste
- 1 tbsp olive oil

Instructions

1. **Heat Oil:** Place a skillet over medium heat and add the olive oil. Allow it to heat until it shimmers slightly, about 1 minute.
2. **Cook Spinach:** Add the spinach to the skillet. Sauté, stirring occasionally, until the spinach is fully wilted, about 2-3 minutes.
3. **Add Eggs and Feta:** Crack the eggs directly into the skillet on top of the spinach, taking care not to break the yolks. Sprinkle the crumbled feta around the eggs. Cover the skillet with a lid and cook until the egg whites are fully set, about 4-5 minutes.
4. **Season & Serve:** Remove the skillet from heat. Season with salt and pepper to taste, and serve the eggs and spinach warm.

Nutritional Breakdown (Estimated per serving)
Calories: 220 kcal, Protein: 14 g, Fat: 16 g, Carbs: 3 g

Tomato & Basil Scrambled Eggs

 Prep Time: 5 minutes *Cook Time: 10 minutes* *Total Time: 15 minutes*
 Yield: 2 servings

Ingredients

- 2 large eggs
- ¼ cup cherry tomatoes, halved
- 1 tbsp fresh basil, chopped
- Salt and pepper, to taste
- 1 tbsp olive oil

Instructions

1. **Heat Oil:** Add olive oil to a skillet and warm over medium heat until it begins to shimmer, about 1 minute.
2. **Cook Tomatoes:** Add the halved cherry tomatoes to the skillet. Sauté, stirring occasionally, until the tomatoes start to soften and release juices, about 3 minutes.
3. **Add Eggs and Basil:** Crack the eggs into the skillet and add the chopped basil. Stir constantly with a spatula, gently folding the eggs and tomatoes until the eggs are scrambled and cooked through, about 3-4 minutes.
4. **Season & Serve:** Season with salt and pepper to taste. Transfer the scrambled eggs to a plate and serve warm.

Nutritional Breakdown (Estimated per serving)
Calories: 200 kcal, Protein: 12 g, Fat: 14 g, Carbs: 5 g

Avocado & Smoked Salmon Breakfast Bowl

 Prep Time: 5 minutes Cook Time: 10 minutes Total Time: 15 minutes

Yield: 2 servings

Ingredients

- 2 large eggs
- ½ ripe avocado, diced
- ¼ cup smoked salmon, chopped
- Salt and pepper, to taste
- 1 tbsp olive oil

Instructions

1. **Heat Oil:** In a skillet, warm the olive oil over medium heat until it begins to shimmer.
2. **Cook Eggs:** Crack the eggs directly into the skillet. Cover with a lid and cook until the whites are completely set and yolks are still soft, about 4 minutes for sunny-side up eggs.
3. **Assemble Bowl:** Place the eggs in a bowl. Top with the diced avocado and chopped smoked salmon.
4. **Season & Serve:** Season with salt and pepper to taste. Serve immediately while warm.

Nutritional Breakdown (Estimated per serving)

Calories: 300 kcal, Protein: 18 g, Fat: 20 g, Carbs: 6 g

Sweet Potato & Sausage Hash

 Prep Time: 5 minutes Cook Time: 15 minutes Total Time: 20 minutes

Yield: 2 servings

Ingredients

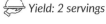

- 1 small sweet potato, diced into ½-inch cubes
- ½ cup sausage, sliced
- Salt and pepper, to taste
- 1 tbsp olive oil

Instructions

1. **Heat Oil:** In a large skillet, warm the olive oil over medium heat until it shimmers.
2. **Cook Sweet Potato and Sausage:** Add the diced sweet potato and sausage slices. Cook, stirring occasionally, until the sweet potato is tender and lightly browned, and the sausage is fully cooked, about 10- 12 minutes.
3. **Season & Serve:** Season the hash with salt and pepper to taste. Serve warm directly from the skillet.

Nutritional Breakdown (Estimated per serving)

Calories: 350 kcal, Protein: 16 g, Fat: 22 g, Carbs: 20 g

Kale & Parmesan Breakfast Scramble

 Prep Time: 5 minutes Cook Time: 10 minutes Total Time: 15 minutes
 Yield: 2 servings

Ingredients

- 2 large eggs
- 1 cup chopped kale, tough stems removed
- 2 tbsp grated Parmesan cheese
- Salt and pepper, to taste
- 1 tbsp olive oil

Instructions

1. **Heat Oil:** Warm olive oil in a skillet over medium heat until it shimmers.
2. **Cook Kale:** Add the chopped kale to the skillet, stirring occasionally until it wilts and becomes tender, about 3 minutes.
3. **Add Eggs and Parmesan:** Crack the eggs into the skillet and sprinkle with Parmesan. Stir gently until the eggs are fully scrambled and set, about 3-4 minutes
4. **Season & Serve:** Season with salt and pepper. Serve the scramble immediately.

Nutritional Breakdown (Estimated per serving)
Calories: 250 kcal, Protein: 14 g, Fat: 18 g, Carbs: 5 g

Mushroom & Goat Cheese Omelet

 Prep Time: 5 minutes Cook Time: 10 minutes Total Time: 15 minutes
 Yield: 1 serving

Ingredients

- 2 large eggs
- ¼ cup sliced mushrooms
- 1 tbsp crumbled goat cheese
- Salt and pepper, to taste
- 1 tbsp olive oil

Instructions

1. **Heat Oil:** Warm olive oil in a skillet over medium heat until it shimmers.
2. **Cook Mushrooms:** Add the sliced mushrooms and cook, stirring occasionally, until tender and golden, about 4 minutes.
3. **Add Eggs and Cheese:** Pour whisked eggs into the skillet. Let the edges set slightly, then add the crumbled goat cheese. Cook until eggs are fully set, about 3 minutes.
4. **Season & Serve:** Season with salt and pepper. Fold the omelet in half and serve warm.

Nutritional Breakdown (Estimated per serving)
Calories: 200 kcal, Protein: 14 g, Fat: 16 g, Carbs: 2 g

Apple Cinnamon Oat Skillet

 Prep Time: 5 minutes *Cook Time: 10 minutes* *Total Time: 15 minutes*
 Yield: 2 servings

Ingredients

- ½ cup rolled oats
- ½ apple, diced
- ¼ tsp cinnamon
- 1 tbsp almond butter
- ¼ cup almond milk

Instructions

1. **Cook Oats and Apple:** In a medium skillet, combine the oats, almond milk, and diced apple. Place over medium heat and cook, stirring occasionally, until the oats are soft and the apple is tender, about 5 minutes.
2. **Add Cinnamon and Almond Butter:** Sprinkle in the cinnamon and swirl in the almond butter. Stir to combine.
3. **Serve:** Remove from heat and enjoy warm directly from the skillet or transfer to bowls.

Nutritional Breakdown (Estimated per serving)

Calories: 270 kcal, Protein: 6 g, Fat: 10 g, Carbs: 42 g

Zucchini & Cheese Egg Bake

 Prep Time: 5 minutes *Cook Time: 15 minutes* *Total Time: 20 minutes*
 Yield: 2 servings

Ingredients

- 2 large eggs
- ½ cup shredded zucchini, moisture squeezed out
- 2 tbsp grated cheese (Parmesan or cheddar)
- Salt and pepper, to taste

Instructions

1. **Prepare Bake:** Preheat your oven to 375°F (190°C). Grease a small baking dish with cooking spray or a light coating of oil.
2. **Mix Ingredients:** In a bowl, whisk the eggs. Add the shredded zucchini and cheese, stirring until well combined. Season with salt and pepper to taste.
3. **Bake:** Pour the mixture into the prepared baking dish. Bake for 15 minutes or until the eggs are set and the top is lightly golden.
4. **Cool & Serve:** Allow to cool for 2 minutes before slicing. Serve warm.

Nutritional Breakdown (Estimated per serving)

Calories: 230 kcal, Protein: 12 g, Fat: 16 g, Carbs: 6 g

Bell Pepper Egg-in-a-Hole

 Prep Time: 5 minutes Cook Time: 10 minutes Total Time: 15 minutes

 Yield: 2 servings

Ingredients

- 1 large bell pepper, cut into ½-inch rings (2 rings)
- 2 large eggs
- Salt and pepper, to taste
- 1 tbsp olive oil

Instructions

1. **Heat Oil:** In a medium skillet over medium heat, warm the olive oil until it shimmers, about 1 minute.
2. **Cook Bell Pepper Rings:** Place the bell pepper rings in the skillet and cook for 1-2 minutes on each side, until they start to soften slightly.
3. **Add Eggs:** Crack an egg into the center of each bell pepper ring. Cover the skillet and cook until the egg whites are fully set, about 3-4 minutes.
4. **Season & Serve:** Sprinkle with salt and pepper to taste. Serve warm.

Nutritional Breakdown (Estimated per serving)

Calories: 180 kcal, Protein: 10 g, Fat: 14 g, Carbs: 4 g

Blueberry Almond Pancake

 Prep Time: 5 minutes Cook Time: 10 minutes Total Time: 15 minutes

 Yield: 2 servings

Ingredients

- ½ cup almond flour
- 1 egg
- ¼ cup almond milk
- ¼ cup fresh blueberries
- 1 tsp vanilla extract

Instructions

1. **Prepare Batter:** In a medium bowl, whisk together almond flour, egg, almond milk, and vanilla extract until smooth. Gently fold in the blueberries.
2. **Cook Pancake:** Heat a non-stick skillet over medium heat. Pour the batter into the skillet, spreading it evenly to form a pancake. Cook for 4-5 minutes on each side, or until golden brown and cooked through.
3. **Serve:** Slice into wedges and serve warm.

Nutritional Breakdown (Estimated per serving)

Calories: 210 kcal, Protein: 8 g, Fat: 14 g, Carbs: 18 g

Greek Yogurt & Egg Breakfast Skillet

 Prep Time: 5 minutes *Cook Time: 10 minutes* *Total Time: 15 minutes*

 Yield: 2 servings

Ingredients

- ½ cup Greek yogurt
- 2 large eggs
- ¼ cup cherry tomatoes, halved
- 1 tbsp olive oil
- Salt and pepper, to taste

Instructions

1. **Heat Oil:** Add olive oil to a skillet and heat over medium. Allow oil to warm for about 1 minute until it shimmers.
2. **Cook Tomatoes and Eggs:** Add the halved cherry tomatoes to the skillet, cooking until softened, about 3 minutes. Crack eggs into the skillet on top of the tomatoes, cover with a lid, and cook until the whites are set, about 4 minutes.
3. **Assemble:** Remove the skillet from heat. Add a dollop of Greek yogurt alongside the eggs and tomatoes in the skillet.
4. **Season & Serve:** Season with salt and pepper to taste. Serve immediately while warm.

Nutritional Breakdown (Estimated per serving)

Calories: 240 kcal, Protein: 16 g, Fat: 14 g, Carbs: 8 g

Sautéed Kale & Turkey Bacon Scramble

 Prep Time: 5 minutes *Cook Time: 10 minutes* *Total Time: 15 minutes*

 Yield: 2 servings

Ingredients

- 2 slices turkey bacon, chopped
- 1 cup chopped kale, stems removed
- 2 large eggs
- 1 tbsp olive oil
- Salt and pepper, to taste

Instructions

1. **Heat Oil:** Warm olive oil in a skillet over medium heat until it begins to shimmer, about 1 minute.
2. **Cook Turkey Bacon:** Add the chopped turkey bacon to the skillet and cook, stirring occasionally, until the bacon is crisp, about 3 minutes.
3. **Add Kale and Eggs:** Add the kale, stirring until it wilts, about 2 minutes. Crack the eggs directly into the skillet and scramble, stirring constantly until eggs are fully cooked, about 3 minutes.
4. **Season & Serve:** Season with salt and pepper to taste. Serve immediately.

Nutritional Breakdown (Estimated per serving)

Calories: 230 kcal, Protein: 15 g, Fat: 16 g, Carbs: 5 g

Cottage Cheese & Avocado Toast

 Prep Time: 5 minutes Cook Time: 10 minutes Total Time: 15 minutes

 Yield: 2 servings

Ingredients

- 1 slice whole-grain bread, toasted
- ½ avocado, mashed
- ¼ cup cottage cheese
- Salt and pepper, to taste

Instructions

1. **Prepare Toast:** Spread the mashed avocado evenly over the toasted bread.
2. **Add Cottage Cheese:** Spoon the cottage cheese on top of the avocado, spreading it evenly.
3. **Season & Serve:** Sprinkle with salt and pepper to taste. Serve immediately.

Nutritional Breakdown (Estimated per serving)
Calories: 220 kcal, Protein: 12 g, Fat: 14 g, Carbs: 12 g

Banana Almond Butter Pancakes

 Prep Time: 5 minutes Cook Time: 10 minutes Total Time: 15 minutes

 Yield: 2 servings

Ingredients

- 1 ripe banana, mashed
- 1 large egg
- 1 tbsp almond butter
- ¼ cup almond flour

Instructions

1. **Prepare Batter:** In a bowl, whisk together the mashed banana, egg, almond butter, and almond flour until smooth and fully combined. **Cook**
2. **Cook Pancakes:** Heat a non-stick skillet over medium heat. Pour small portions of the batter into the skillet to form pancakes. Cook each pancake for 3-4 minutes on each side until golden brown and fully set.
3. **Serve:** Transfer pancakes to a plate and enjoy warm.

Nutritional Breakdown (Estimated per serving)
Calories: 260 kcal, Protein: 8 g, Fat: 14 g, Carbs: 28 g

One-Pan Ham & Cheese Breakfast Roll-Up

 Prep Time: 5 minutes *Cook Time: 10 minutes* *Total Time: 15 minutes*

 Yield: 1 serving

Ingredients

- 1 large egg, beaten
- 1 slice ham
- ¼ cup shredded cheese (cheddar or mozzarella)
- 1 tbsp butter

Instructions

1. **Melt Butter:** Add butter to a skillet and melt over medium heat.
2. **Cook Egg:** Pour the beaten egg into the skillet, spreading it out to form an even layer. Let cook until set, about 2 minutes.
3. **Add Ham and Cheese:** Place the slice of ham on top of the cooked egg and sprinkle with cheese. Continue cooking until the cheese begins to melt, about 2-3 minutes.
4. **Roll & Serve:** Carefully roll up the egg, ham, and cheese into a log. Slice if desired and serve warm.

Nutritional Breakdown (Estimated per serving)

Calories: 280 kcal, Protein: 16 g, Fat: 18 g, Carbs: 6 g

Spicy Egg & Turkey Sausage Skillet

 Prep Time: 5 minutes *Cook Time: 10 minutes* *Total Time: 15 minutes*

 Yield: 2 servings

Ingredients

- 2 turkey sausages, sliced
- 2 large eggs
- ¼ tsp red pepper flakes
- Salt and pepper, to taste
- 1 tbsp olive oil

Instructions

1. **Heat Oil:** Add olive oil to a skillet and heat over medium until it shimmers.
2. **Cook Sausage:** Add the sliced turkey sausage to the skillet and cook, stirring occasionally, until browned, about 3 minutes.
3. **Add Eggs and Spice:** Crack the eggs into the skillet, sprinkle with red pepper flakes, and cover. Cook until the eggs are set to your preference, about 4 minutes.
4. **Season & Serve:** Season with salt and pepper to taste and serve immediately.

Nutritional Breakdown (Estimated per serving)

Calories: 250 kcal, Protein: 18 g, Fat: 16 g, Carbs: 4 g

Coconut Chia Pudding with Berries

 Prep Time: 5 minutes *Cook Time: 20 minutes* *Total Time: 25 minutes*

Yield: 2 servings

Ingredients

- ¼ cup chia seeds
- 1 cup coconut milk
- ½ cup mixed berries

Instructions

1. **Combine Ingredients:** In a medium bowl, stir together chia seeds and coconut milk until well combined.
2. **Chill:** Cover the bowl and refrigerate for at least 20 minutes, or until the mixture thickens to a pudding-like consistency.
3. **Serve:** Top with mixed berries and serve chilled.

Nutritional Breakdown (Estimated per serving)
Calories: 180 kcal, Protein: 6 g, Fat: 10 g, Carbs: 18 g

Savory Egg & Avocado Quesadilla

 Prep Time: 5 minutes *Cook Time: 10 minutes* *Total Time: 15 minutes*

Yield: 1 serving

Ingredients

- 1 large egg, scrambled
- 1 small whole-grain tortilla
- ¼ avocado, sliced
- ¼ cup shredded cheese
- 1 tbsp olive oil

Instructions

1. **Heat Oil:** Warm olive oil in a skillet over medium heat.
2. **Cook Egg:** Scramble the egg in the skillet until fully cooked. Remove the egg and set aside.
3. **Assemble Quesadilla:** Place the tortilla in the skillet. Layer with scrambled egg, cheese, and avocado slices. Fold the tortilla in half.
4. **Cook Quesadilla:** Cook each side for 2-3 minutes, until golden brown and cheese has melted.
5. **Serve:** Cut into wedges and serve warm.

Nutritional Breakdown (Estimated per serving)
Calories: 300 kcal, Protein: 12 g, Fat: 20 g, Carbs: 18 g

Smoked Salmon & Spinach Breakfast Wrap

 Prep Time: 5 minutes *Cook Time: 5 minutes* *Total Time: 10 minutes*

 Yield: 1 serving

Ingredients

- 1 small whole-grain wrap
- ¼ cup smoked salmon, thinly sliced
- ½ cup fresh spinach leaves
- 1 tbsp cream cheese

Instructions

1. **Spread Cream Cheese:** Place the wrap on a flat surface. Use a spoon or butter knife to spread the cream cheese evenly over the wrap.
2. **Assemble Wrap:** Lay the smoked salmon slices and fresh spinach leaves evenly over the cream cheese.
3. **Roll Up:** Starting at one end, roll the wrap tightly into a cylinder. Slice in half if desired.
4. **Serve:** Enjoy immediately or wrap in foil for an easy, on-the-go breakfast.

Nutritional Breakdown (Estimated per serving)

Calories: 250 kcal, Protein: 15 g, Fat: 12 g, Carbs: 15 g

Cinnamon Ricotta & Honey Toast

 Prep Time: 5 minutes *Cook Time: 5 minutes* *Total Time: 10 minutes*

 Yield: 1 serving

Ingredients

- 1 slice whole-grain bread, toasted
- ¼ cup ricotta cheese
- ½ tsp ground cinnamon
- 1 tsp honey

Instructions

1. **Prepare Toast:** Place the toasted bread on a plate and use a spoon to spread the ricotta cheese evenly over the top.
2. **Add Cinnamon and Honey:** Sprinkle the cinnamon evenly over the ricotta layer. Drizzle the honey over the top.
3. **Serve:** Serve immediately as an open-faced toast. Enjoy warm for a sweet, protein-rich breakfast.

Nutritional Breakdown (Estimated per serving)

Calories: 200 kcal, Protein: 8 g, Fat: 10 g, Carbs: 20 g

Quick Lemon Herb Chicken Bowl

 Prep Time: 5 minutes *Cook Time: 15 minutes* *Total Time: 20 minutes* *Yield: 2 servings*

Ingredients

- 2 boneless, skinless chicken breasts, cut into 1-inch cubes
- 1 tbsp olive oil
- 1 tbsp lemon juice
- ½ tsp dried oregano
- Salt and pepper, to taste
- 1 cup quinoa, cooked according to package instructions

Instructions

1. **Heat Oil:** Place a large skillet over medium heat and add the olive oil. Allow it to heat until it shimmers, about 1 minute.
2. **Season Chicken:** While the skillet heats, season the cubed chicken with lemon juice, oregano, salt, and pepper. Toss to coat evenly.
3. **Cook Chicken:** Add the seasoned chicken to the skillet in a single layer. Let it cook undisturbed for 3-4 minutes to develop a golden crust. Stir and continue cooking, stirring occasionally, until chicken is cooked through and golden, about 12-15 minutes.
4. **Assemble Bowl:** Divide the cooked quinoa into two bowls and top with the cooked chicken. Serve immediately.

> *Nutritional Breakdown (Estimated per serving)*
> Calories: 350 kcal, Protein: 26 g, Fat: 15 g, Carbs: 22 g

Garlic Shrimp & Spinach Stir-Fry

 Prep Time: 5 minutes *Cook Time: 10 minutes* *Total Time: 15 minutes* *Yield: 2 servings*

Ingredients

- 1 cup raw shrimp, peeled and deveined
- 2 cups fresh spinach
- 1 tbsp olive oil
- 1 clove garlic, minced
- Salt and pepper, to taste

Instructions

1. **Heat Oil:** In a large skillet over medium heat, add the olive oil and heat until shimmering, about 1 minute.
2. **Cook Garlic and Shrimp:** Add the minced garlic to the skillet and sauté until fragrant, about 30 seconds. Add the shrimp in a single layer and season with salt and pepper. Cook until pink and opaque, about 2 minutes per side.
3. **Add Spinach:** Add the spinach to the skillet and toss with the shrimp, cooking until wilted, about 2 minutes.
4. **Serve:** Divide the shrimp and spinach between two plates and serve immediately.

> *Nutritional Breakdown (Estimated per serving)*
> Calories: 280 kcal, Protein: 22 g, Fat: 14 g, Carbs: 12 g

Spicy Chicken & Veggie Lettuce Wraps

 Prep Time: 5 minutes Cook Time: 15 minutes Total Time: 20 minutes
 Yield: 2 servings

Ingredients

- 2 boneless, skinless chicken breasts, finely diced
- 1 tbsp olive oil
- ½ bell pepper, finely diced
- 1 tsp chili powder
- Salt and pepper, to taste
- 4 large lettuce leaves

Instructions

1. **Heat Oil:** Add olive oil to a skillet and heat over medium. Allow the oil to warm for about 1 minute.
2. **Cook Chicken and Bell Pepper:** Add the diced chicken to the skillet, season with chilli powder, salt, and pepper, and cook, stirring frequently, until chicken is no longer pink, about 5-7 minutes. Add the diced bell pepper and cook for an additional 3-4 minutes until tender.
3. **Assemble Wraps:** Spoon the cooked chicken and pepper mixture into the center of each lettuce leaf.
4. **Serve:** Fold the lettuce leaves around the filling and enjoy immediately.

Nutritional Breakdown (Estimated per serving)

Calories: 320 kcal, Protein: 24 g, Fat: 16 g, Carbs: 14 g

Turkey & Zucchini Skillet

 Prep Time: 5 minutes Cook Time: 15 minutes Total Time: 20 minutes
Yield: 2 servings

Ingredients

- 1 cup ground turkey
- 1 medium zucchini, diced
- 1 tbsp olive oil
- Salt and pepper, to taste

Instructions

1. **Heat Oil:** In a skillet over medium heat, add the olive oil and warm until shimmering, about 1 minute.
2. **Cook Turkey:** Add ground turkey to the skillet, breaking it apart with a spatula. Season with salt and pepper, and cook, stirring frequently, until browned and cooked through, about 7-8 minutes.
3. **Add Zucchini:** Add the diced zucchini to the skillet, stirring to combine. Cook for another 5-7 minutes until the zucchini is tender.
4. **Serve:** Divide between two plates and serve warm.

Nutritional Breakdown (Estimated per serving)

Calories: 300 kcal, Protein: 22 g, Fat: 14 g, Carbs: 10 g

Lemon Garlic Salmon & Asparagus

 Prep Time: 5 minutes *Cook Time: 15 minutes* *Total Time: 20 minutes*
 Yield: 2 servings

Ingredients

- 2 salmon fillets (4 oz each)
- 1 tbsp olive oil
- 1 clove garlic, minced
- 1 tbsp lemon juice
- 1 cup asparagus, trimmed
- Salt and pepper, to taste

Instructions

1. **Heat Oil:** Warm olive oil in a skillet over medium heat until shimmering, about 1 minute.
2. **Cook Salmon:** Season the salmon with salt, pepper, and lemon juice. Place in the skillet, skin side down, and cook for 4-5 minutes per side, until salmon flakes easily with a fork. Remove salmon from the skillet and set aside.
3. **Sauté Asparagus:** Add garlic and asparagus to the skillet and cook, stirring occasionally, until tender-crisp, about 5 minutes.
4. **Serve:** Plate the salmon and asparagus together and serve immediately.

Nutritional Breakdown (Estimated per serving)
Calories: 320 kcal, Protein: 26 g, Fat: 18 g, Carbs: 8 g

Ground Beef & Broccoli Stir-Fry

 Prep Time: 5 minutes *Cook Time: 15 minutes* *Total Time: 20 minutes*
 Yield: 2 servings

Ingredients

- 1 cup ground beef
- 1 cup broccoli florets
- 1 tbsp olive oil
- 1 tbsp soy sauce
- Salt and pepper, to taste

Instructions

1. **Heat Oil:** Warm olive oil in a large skillet over medium heat.
2. **Cook Beef:** Add ground beef, season with salt and pepper, and cook, breaking it up with a spatula, until fully browned, about 7-8 minutes.
3. **Add Broccoli:** Add broccoli florets and soy sauce to the skillet. Stir to combine, then cover and cook for 5-7 minutes, until broccoli is tender but still bright green.
4. **Serve:** Divide between plates and serve warm.

Nutritional Breakdown (Estimated per serving)
Calories: 330 kcal, Protein: 24 g, Fat: 18 g, Carbs: 12 g

Herbed Chicken & Veggie Stir-Fry

 Prep Time: 5 minutes Cook Time: 15 minutes Total Time: 20 minutes

 Yield: 2 servings

Ingredients

- 2 boneless, skinless chicken thighs, sliced
- 1 cup bell pepper, sliced
- 1 cup zucchini, sliced
- 1 tbsp olive oil
- 1 tsp dried Italian herbs
- Salt and pepper, to taste

Instructions

1. **Heat Oil:** Add olive oil to a skillet and warm over medium heat.
2. **Cook Chicken:** Add sliced chicken to the skillet, season with Italian herbs, salt, and pepper, and cook, stirring frequently, until browned, about 7-8 minutes.
3. **Add Veggies:** Add bell pepper and zucchini to the skillet, stirring to combine. Cook for an additional 5-7 minutes until vegetables are tender-crisp.
4. **Serve:** Divide between plates and serve warm.

Nutritional Breakdown (Estimated per serving)
Calories: 320 kcal, Protein: 24 g, Fat: 14 g, Carbs: 18 g

Egg & Turkey Sausage Zoodle Bowl

 Prep Time: 5 minutes Cook Time: 10 minutes Total Time: 15 minutes

 Yield: 2 servings

Ingredients

- 2 turkey sausages, sliced
- 2 large eggs
- 2 cups zucchini noodles (zoodles)
- 1 tbsp olive oil
- Salt and pepper, to taste

Instructions

1. **Heat Oil:** In a skillet over medium heat, add olive oil and warm until shimmering.
2. **Cook Sausages and Eggs:** Add sliced turkey sausages and cook for 3-4 minutes. Push to one side and crack eggs into the skillet. Cook until whites are set, about 4 minutes.
3. **Add Zoodles:** Add zucchini noodles to the skillet, tossing gently for about 1-2 minutes until just softened.
4. **Serve:** Transfer to bowls and enjoy warm.

Nutritional Breakdown (Estimated per serving)
Calories: 280 kcal, Protein: 18 g, Fat: 14 g, Carbs: 8 g

Sesame Chicken & Snow Pea Stir-Fry

 Prep Time: 5 minutes Cook Time: 15 minutes Total Time: 20 minutes
 Yield: 2 servings

Ingredients

- 2 boneless, skinless chicken breasts, thinly sliced
- 1 cup snow peas
- 1 tbsp olive oil
- 1 tbsp sesame oil
- 1 tbsp soy sauce
- 1 tsp sesame seeds
- Salt and pepper, to taste

Instructions

1. **Heat Oils:** Place a large skillet over medium heat and add the olive oil and sesame oil. Allow the oils to heat until shimmering, about 1 minute.
2. **Cook Chicken:** Add the sliced chicken to the skillet in a single layer. Season with salt and pepper. Cook undisturbed for 3-4 minutes, allowing the chicken to brown. Stir and cook for another 5-6 minutes, until fully cooked and no longer pink in the center.
3. **Add Snow Peas and Soy Sauce:** Add the snow peas to the skillet, pour in the soy sauce, and stir to coat everything evenly. Cook for another 3-4 minutes until the snow peas are bright green and tender-crisp.
4. **Serve:** Sprinkle sesame seeds over the stir-fry. Divide between plates and serve immediately.

Nutritional Breakdown (Estimated per serving)
Calories: 320 kcal, Protein: 26 g, Fat: 14 g, Carbs: 14 g

Lemon Garlic Shrimp & Asparagus

 Prep Time: 5 minutes Cook Time: 10 minutes Total Time: 15 minutes
 Yield: 2 servings

Ingredients

- 1 cup large shrimp, peeled and deveined
- 1 cup asparagus, trimmed and cut into 1-inch pieces
- 1 tbsp olive oil
- 1 tbsp lemon juice
- 1 clove garlic, minced
- Salt and pepper, to taste

Instructions

1. **Heat Oil:** Warm the olive oil in a large skillet over medium heat until shimmering, about 1 minute.
2. **Cook Garlic and Shrimp:** Add the minced garlic to the skillet and cook until fragrant, about 30 seconds. Add the shrimp in a single layer, season with salt and pepper, and cook for 2-3 minutes on each side, until pink and opaque.
3. **Add Asparagus and Lemon Juice:** Add the asparagus and lemon juice to the skillet. Cook, stirring occasionally, until the asparagus is tender-crisp and bright green, about 3-4 minutes.
4. **Serve:** Transfer to plates and serve immediately while warm.

Nutritional Breakdown (Estimated per serving)
Calories: 250 kcal, Protein: 18 g, Fat: 12 g, Carbs: 8 g

Beef & Bell Pepper Fajita Bowl

 Prep Time: 5 minutes Cook Time: 15 minutes Total Time: 20 minutes

 Yield: 2 servings

Ingredients

- 1 cup thinly sliced beef strips
- 1 red bell pepper, sliced
- 1 green bell pepper, sliced
- 1 tbsp olive oil
- ½ tsp cumin
- Salt and pepper, to taste

Instructions

1. **Heat Oil:** Place a large skillet over medium-high heat and add the olive oil. Let it heat until shimmering, about 1 minute.
2. **Cook Beef:** Add the beef strips to the skillet, season with cumin, salt, and pepper, and cook undisturbed for 3-4 minutes to allow browning. Stir and continue cooking for another 4-5 minutes until the beef is fully cooked and tender.
3. **Add Bell Peppers:** Add the bell pepper slices to the skillet. Cook, stirring frequently, until the peppers are tender, about 5 minutes.
4. **Serve:** Divide the beef and bell pepper mixture between two bowls and serve warm.

Nutritional Breakdown (Estimated per serving)

Calories: 350 kcal, Protein: 24 g, Fat: 16 g, Carbs: 18 g

Turkey & Veggie Skillet

 Prep Time: 5 minutes Cook Time: 15 minutes Total Time: 20 minutes

 Yield: 2 servings

Ingredients

- 1 cup ground turkey
- 1 zucchini, diced
- 1 yellow squash, diced
- 1 tbsp olive oil
- Salt and pepper, to taste

Instructions

1. **Heat Oil:** In a large skillet, warm olive oil over medium heat until shimmering, about 1 minute.
2. **Cook Turkey:** Add ground turkey to the skillet, season with salt and pepper, and cook, breaking it apart with a spatula, until browned and cooked through, about 7-8 minutes.
3. **Add Vegetables:** Add diced zucchini and yellow squash to the skillet, stirring to combine with the turkey. Cook, stirring occasionally, until the vegetables are tender, about 5-7 minutes.
4. **Serve:** Divide between plates and enjoy warm.

Nutritional Breakdown (Estimated per serving)

Calories: 300 kcal, Protein: 22 g, Fat: 14 g, Carbs: 12 g

Garlic Mushroom & Chicken Stir-Fry

 Prep Time: 5 minutes Cook Time: 15 minutes Total Time: 20 minutes

Yield: 2 servings

Ingredients

- 2 boneless, skinless chicken breasts, cut into 1-inch cubes
- 1 cup sliced mushrooms
- 1 tbsp olive oil
- 1 clove garlic, minced
- Salt and pepper, to taste

Instructions

1. **Heat Oil:** Add olive oil to a large skillet and heat over medium until it shimmers, about 1 minute.
2. **Cook Garlic and Chicken:** Add the minced garlic and chicken cubes to the skillet. Stir to coat the chicken with oil and garlic, and season with salt and pepper. Cook, stirring occasionally, until the chicken is golden and cooked through, about 7-8 minutes.
3. **Add Mushrooms:** Add the sliced mushrooms to the skillet and stir to combine. Cook until the mushrooms are tender and have released their juices, about 5 minutes.
4. **Serve:** Transfer to plates and serve warm.

Nutritional Breakdown (Estimated per serving)
Calories: 320 kcal, Protein: 24 g, Fat: 14 g, Carbs: 10 g

Cajun Salmon & Spinach Sauté

 Prep Time: 5 minutes Cook Time: 10 minutes Total Time: 15 minutes

Yield: 2 servings

Ingredients

- 2 salmon fillets (4 oz each)
- 1 tsp Cajun seasoning
- 1 tbsp olive oil
- 2 cups fresh spinach
- Salt and pepper, to taste

Instructions

1. **Heat Oil:** Place a skillet over medium heat and add the olive oil, letting it warm until shimmering, about 1 minute.
2. **Cook Salmon:** Season each salmon fillet with Cajun seasoning, salt, and pepper. Place the salmon in the skillet, skin-side down, and cook for 4-5 minutes on each side, until it flakes easily with a fork. Remove salmon from the skillet and set aside.
3. **Sauté Spinach:** Add spinach to the skillet, stirring until wilted, about 2 minutes.
4. **Serve:** Plate the salmon alongside the spinach and serve warm.

Nutritional Breakdown (Estimated per serving)
Calories: 300 kcal, Protein: 22 g, Fat: 18 g, Carbs: 6 g

Zesty Lime Chicken & Avocado Salad

 Prep Time: 5 minutes *Cook Time: 10 minutes* *Total Time: 15 minutes*

 Yield: 2 servings

Ingredients

- 2 boneless, skinless chicken breasts
- 1 tbsp olive oil
- 1 tbsp lime juice
- Salt and pepper, to taste
- 1 avocado, sliced

Instructions

1. **Heat Oil:** In a large skillet, warm olive oil over medium heat until it shimmers, about 1 minute.
2. **Cook Chicken:** Season chicken breasts with lime juice, salt, and pepper. Place in the skillet and cook for 5-6 minutes per side until golden and fully cooked. Remove chicken from the skillet and allow it to rest for a minute before slicing.
3. **Assemble Salad:** Divide avocado slices between two plates and top each plate with the sliced chicken.
4. **Serve:** Enjoy immediately.

Nutritional Breakdown (Estimated per serving)
Calories: 320 kcal, Protein: 24 g, Fat: 18 g, Carbs: 8 g

Teriyaki Turkey & Vegetable Stir-Fry

 Prep Time: 5 minutes *Cook Time: 15 minutes* *Total Time: 20 minutes*

 Yield: 2 servings

Ingredients

- 1 cup ground turkey
- 1 cup bell peppers, sliced (any color)
- 1 tbsp olive oil
- 1 tbsp teriyaki sauce
- Salt and pepper, to taste

Instructions

1. **Heat Oil:** In a large skillet, add olive oil and heat over medium until it shimmers, about 1 minute.
2. **Cook Turkey:** Add the ground turkey to the skillet, season with salt and pepper, and cook, breaking it up with a spatula, until browned and fully cooked, about 7-8 minutes.
3. **Add Vegetables and Teriyaki Sauce:** Add the bell pepper slices and teriyaki sauce to the skillet. Stir to combine and cook for another 5 minutes, until the peppers are tender-crisp.
4. **Serve:** Divide between plates and enjoy immediately.

Nutritional Breakdown (Estimated per serving)
Calories: 330 kcal, Protein: 24 g, Fat: 14 g, Carbs: 20 g

Italian Chicken & Tomato Sauté

 Prep Time: 5 minutes *Cook Time: 15 minutes* *Total Time: 20 minutes*
 Yield: 2 servings

Ingredients

- 2 boneless, skinless chicken breasts, cut into 1-inch pieces
- 1 cup cherry tomatoes, halved
- 1 tbsp olive oil
- 1 tsp Italian seasoning
- Salt and pepper, to taste

Instructions

1. **Heat Oil:** Add olive oil to a skillet and heat over medium until it shimmers, about 1 minute.
2. **Cook Chicken:** Add the chicken pieces to the skillet, season with Italian seasoning, salt, and pepper. Spread chicken in a single layer and cook undisturbed for 3-4 minutes until the underside is golden brown. Stir and cook for an additional 4-5 minutes, until cooked through.
3. **Add Tomatoes:** Add the halved cherry tomatoes to the skillet. Stir gently and cook for 3-4 minutes, until the tomatoes soften and release juices.
4. **Serve:** Divide between plates and serve warm.

Nutritional Breakdown (Estimated per serving)

Calories: 320 kcal, Protein: 26 g, Fat: 16 g, Carbs: 8 g

Honey Mustard Salmon & Zucchini

 Prep Time: 5 minutes *Cook Time: 10 minutes* *Total Time: 15 minutes*
 Yield: 2 servings

Ingredients

- 2 salmon fillets (4 oz each)
- 1 tbsp honey
- 1 tbsp Dijon mustard
- 1 medium zucchini, sliced
- 1 tbsp olive oil
- Salt and pepper, to taste

Instructions

1. **Prepare Honey Mustard Sauce:** In a small bowl, mix honey and Dijon mustard until smooth. Set aside.
2. **Heat Oil:** In a large skillet, heat olive oil over medium heat until it shimmers, about 1 minute.
3. **Cook Salmon:** Season the salmon fillets with salt and pepper. Place in the skillet, skin-side down, and cook for 4-5 minutes per side, until the salmon flakes easily with a fork. Remove from skillet and brush with honey mustard sauce.
4. **Cook Zucchini:** In the same skillet, add zucchini slices. Cook, stirring occasionally, until tender and slightly browned, about 4 minutes.
5. **Serve:** Plate the salmon and zucchini together. Serve warm.

Nutritional Breakdown (Estimated per serving)

Calories: 300 kcal, Protein: 24 g, Fat: 14 g, Carbs: 12 g

Greek Chicken & Cauliflower Rice Bowl

 Prep Time: 5 minutes *Cook Time: 15 minutes* *Total Time: 20 minutes* *Yield: 2 servings*

Ingredients

- 2 boneless, skinless chicken breasts, diced into 1-inch pieces
- 1 tbsp olive oil
- 1 tsp dried oregano
- 1 cup cauliflower rice (store-bought or homemade)
- ½ cup cherry tomatoes, halved
- ¼ cup crumbled feta cheese
- Salt and pepper, to taste

Instructions

1. **Heat Oil:** In a large skillet, add olive oil and heat over medium until it shimmers, about 1 minute.
2. **Cook Chicken:** Add the diced chicken to the skillet and season with oregano, salt, and pepper. Cook, stirring occasionally, until golden and cooked through, about 8-10 minutes.
3. **Add Cauliflower Rice:** Once the chicken is fully cooked, add cauliflower rice to the skillet. Stir to combine and cook for an additional 3-4 minutes until the cauliflower rice is tender.
4. **Assemble Bowl:** Divide the chicken and cauliflower rice between two bowls. Top each bowl with halved cherry tomatoes and sprinkle with feta cheese.
5. **Serve:** Serve immediately while warm.

Nutritional Breakdown (Estimated per serving)

Calories: 280 kcal, Protein: 24 g, Fat: 12 g, Carbs: 12 g

Spicy Beef & Broccoli Stir-Fry

 Prep Time: 5 minutes *Cook Time: 15 minutes* *Total Time: 20 minutes* *Yield: 2 servings*

Ingredients

- 1 cup thinly sliced beef (such as sirloin or flank steak)
- 1 cup broccoli florets
- 1 tbsp olive oil
- 1 tsp sriracha or hot sauce
- 1 tbsp soy sauce
- Salt and pepper, to taste

Instructions

1. **Heat Oil:** In a large skillet or wok, heat olive oil over medium-high heat until it shimmers, about 1 minute.
2. **Cook Beef:** Add the beef slices in a single layer, season with salt and pepper, and cook undisturbed for 2-3 minutes to brown. Stir and cook for another 2-3 minutes until fully browned.
3. **Add Broccoli and Sauces:** Add broccoli florets to the skillet, along with sriracha and soy sauce. Stir well to coat everything in the sauces. Cook, stirring occasionally, until the broccoli is tender but still crisp, about 5-6 minutes.
4. **Serve:** Divide the beef and broccoli stir-fry between plates. Serve warm.

Nutritional Breakdown (Estimated per serving)

Calories: 340 kcal, Protein: 26 g, Fat: 16 g, Carbs: 14 g

CHAPTER 4: DINNER

Rosemary Garlic Steak & Veggie Skillet

 Prep Time: 5 minutes *Cook Time: 15 minutes* *Total Time: 20 minutes*

Yield: 2 servings

Ingredients

- 1 steak (such as sirloin or ribeye), about 8 oz, sliced into 1-inch strips
- 1 cup mixed vegetables (e.g., bell peppers and zucchini), sliced
- 1 tbsp olive oil
- 1 clove garlic, minced
- 1 tsp fresh rosemary, chopped
- Salt and pepper, to taste

Instructions

1. **Heat Oil:** In a large skillet over medium heat, add olive oil and heat until it shimmers, about 1 minute.
2. **Cook Steak:** Add steak strips to the skillet, season with salt, pepper, garlic, and rosemary. Cook for 3-4 minutes, stirring occasionally, until the steak reaches your preferred doneness. Remove the steak from the skillet and set aside.
3. **Cook Vegetables:** In the same skillet, add mixed vegetables and cook for 5-6 minutes until tender-crisp.
4. **Serve:** Divide the steak and vegetables between plates and serve warm.

Nutritional Breakdown (Estimated per serving)
Calories: 400 kcal, Protein: 28 g, Fat: 24 g, Carbs: 12 g

Lemon Herb Chicken & Asparagus

 Prep Time: 5 minutes *Cook Time: 15 minutes* *Total Time: 20 minutes*

 Yield: 2 servings

Ingredients

- 2 boneless, skinless chicken breasts
- 1 tbsp olive oil
- 1 tbsp lemon juice
- 1 tsp fresh thyme or rosemary, chopped
- 1 cup asparagus, trimmed
- Salt and pepper, to taste

Instructions

1. **Heat Oil:** Add olive oil to a skillet and heat over medium until it shimmers, about 1 minute.
2. **Cook Chicken:** Season chicken breasts with lemon juice, thyme, salt, and pepper. Add to the skillet and cook for 5-6 minutes per side until golden and cooked through. Remove from skillet and set aside.
3. **Cook Asparagus:** In the same skillet, add asparagus and cook, stirring occasionally, until tender, about 5 minutes.
4. **Serve:** Plate the chicken with the asparagus and serve warm.

Nutritional Breakdown (Estimated per serving)
Calories: 310 kcal, Protein: 26 g, Fat: 18 g, Carbs: 6 g

Garlic Butter Shrimp & Zoodles

 Prep Time: 5 minutes *Cook Time: 10 minutes* *Total Time: 15 minutes*

 Yield: 2 servings

Ingredients

- 1 cup large shrimp, peeled and deveined
- 2 cups zucchini noodles (zoodles)
- 1 tbsp butter
- 1 clove garlic, minced
- Salt and pepper, to taste

Instructions

1. **Heat Butter:** Melt butter in a skillet over medium heat until it begins to bubble.
2. **Cook Shrimp:** Add minced garlic and shrimp. Season with salt and pepper and cook for 2-3 minutes on each side, until pink and opaque. Remove shrimp and set aside.
3. **Add Zoodles:** In the same skillet, add zoodles and cook for 2-3 minutes, stirring, until tender.
4. **Serve:** Plate the zoodles and top with the shrimp. Serve immediately.

> *Nutritional Breakdown (Estimated per serving)*
> Calories: 280 kcal, Protein: 20 g, Fat: 18 g, Carbs: 8 g

Honey Dijon Salmon & Green Beans

 Prep Time: 5 minutes *Cook Time: 15 minutes* *Total Time: 20 minutes*

 Yield: 2 servings

Ingredients

- 2 salmon fillets (4 oz each)
- 1 tbsp honey
- 1 tbsp Dijon mustard
- 1 cup green beans, trimmed
- 1 tbsp olive oil
- Salt and pepper, to taste

Instructions

1. **Prepare Honey Mustard Sauce:** In a small bowl, mix honey and Dijon mustard until smooth. Set aside.
2. **Heat Oil:** Warm olive oil in a skillet over medium heat.
3. **Cook Salmon:** Season the salmon fillets with salt and pepper. Place in the skillet, skin-side down, and cook for 4-5 minutes per side, until the salmon flakes easily with a fork. Remove and brush with honey mustard sauce.
4. **Cook Green Beans:** Add green beans to the skillet and cook until tender, about 5 minutes.
5. **Serve:** Plate the salmon and green beans together and serve warm.

> *Nutritional Breakdown (Estimated per serving)*
> Calories: 340 kcal, Protein: 24 g, Fat: 18 g, Carbs: 12 g

Spicy Ground Turkey & Cauliflower Rice

 Prep Time: 5 minutes *Cook Time: 15 minutes* *Total Time: 20 minutes*

Yield: 2 servings

Ingredients

- 1 cup ground turkey
- 1 cup cauliflower rice
- 1 tbsp olive oil
- 1 tsp chili powder
- Salt and pepper, to taste

Instructions

1. **Heat Oil:** Add olive oil to a skillet and heat over medium.
2. **Cook Turkey:** Add ground turkey to the skillet, season with chili powder, salt, and pepper. Cook, stirring frequently, until browned and cooked through, about 7-8 minutes.
3. **Add Cauliflower Rice:** Add cauliflower rice to the skillet and cook until tender, about 3-4 minutes.
4. **Serve:** Divide between plates and serve warm.

Nutritional Breakdown (Estimated per serving)
Calories: 300 kcal, Protein: 26 g, Fat: 12 g, Carbs: 12 g

Coconut Curry Shrimp & Spinach

 Prep Time: 5 minutes *Cook Time: 15 minutes* *Total Time: 20 minutes*

Yield: 2 servings

Ingredients

- 1 cup shrimp, peeled and deveined
- 2 cups spinach
- ½ cup coconut milk
- 1 tbsp curry powder
- Salt and pepper, to taste

Instructions

1. **Heat Coconut Milk:** Pour coconut milk into a skillet over medium heat. Stir in curry powder until blended.
2. **Cook Shrimp:** Add shrimp to the skillet, season with salt and pepper, and cook for 3-4 minutes on each side, until pink and cooked through.
3. **Add Spinach:** Stir in spinach and cook until wilted, about 2 minutes.
4. **Serve:** Divide between plates and serve immediately.

Nutritional Breakdown (Estimated per serving)
Calories: 320 kcal, Protein: 18 g, Fat: 16 g, Carbs: 14 g

Balsamic Glazed Chicken & Roasted Carrots

 Prep Time: 5 minutes *Cook Time: 20 minutes* *Total Time: 25 minutes*
 Yield: 2 servings

Ingredients

- 2 chicken breasts
- 1 tbsp balsamic vinegar
- 1 tbsp olive oil
- 1 cup baby carrots
- Salt and pepper, to taste

Instructions

1. **Preheat Oven:** Preheat the oven to 400°F (200°C).
2. **Prepare Chicken and Carrots:** Place chicken and carrots on a baking sheet. Drizzle with balsamic vinegar and olive oil, then season with salt and pepper.
3. **Bake:** Roast for 20 minutes, or until the chicken is cooked through and carrots are tender.
4. **Serve:** Slice the chicken and plate with carrots. Serve warm.

Nutritional Breakdown (Estimated per serving)
Calories: 320 kcal, Protein: 26 g, Fat: 14 g, Carbs: 18 g

Tomato Basil Pasta with Ground Beef

 Prep Time: 5 minutes *Cook Time: 15 minutes* *Total Time: 20 minutes*
 Yield: 2 servings

Ingredients

- 1 cup cooked pasta (such as penne)
- 1 cup ground beef
- 1 cup cherry tomatoes, halved
- 1 tbsp olive oil
- 1 tsp dried basil
- Salt and pepper, to taste

Instructions

1. **Heat Oil:** In a large skillet, add olive oil and heat over medium.
2. **Cook Beef:** Add ground beef, season with salt, pepper, and basil, and cook until browned, about 7-8 minutes.
3. **Add Tomatoes:** Once the beef is browned, add the halved cherry tomatoes to the skillet. Stir and cook for 3-4 minutes until the tomatoes soften and release their juices.
4. **Combine with Pasta:** Add the cooked pasta to the skillet and toss to combine everything thoroughly.
5. **Serve:** Divide the pasta between plates and serve warm, optionally garnished with fresh basil if available.

Nutritional Breakdown (Estimated per serving)
Calories: 360 kcal, Protein: 24 g, Fat: 14 g, Carbs: 26 g

Parmesan-Crusted Pork Chops & Brussels Sprouts

 Prep Time: 5 minutes *Cook Time: 15 minutes* *Total Time: 20 minutes* *Yield: 2 servings*

 Ingredients

- 1 cup ground turkey
- 1 cup ca 2 boneless pork chops
- ¼ cup grated Parmesan cheese
- 1 cup Brussels sprouts, halved
- 1 tbsp olive oil
- Salt and pepper, to taste
- uliflower rice
- 1 tbsp olive oil
- 1 tsp chili powder
- Salt and pepper, to taste

Instructions

1. **Preheat Oven:** Preheat your oven to 400°F (200°C).
2. **Prepare Pork Chops:** Pat pork chops dry and season with salt and pepper. Coat each pork chop in grated Parmesan cheese, pressing lightly to adhere the cheese to the surface.
3. **Cook Pork Chops:** Heat a large, oven-safe skillet over medium heat and add half of the olive oil. Place the pork chops in the skillet and cook for 3-4 minutes on each side until golden.
4. **Add Brussels Sprouts:** Toss Brussels sprouts with remaining olive oil, salt, and pepper, then add them to the skillet around the pork chops.
5. **Bake:** Transfer the skillet to the preheated oven and bake for 8-10 minutes, or until the pork chops are cooked through and Brussels sprouts are tender.
6. **Serve:** Plate the pork chops with Brussels sprouts and serve warm.

Nutritional Breakdown (Estimated per serving)

Calories: 370 kcal, Protein: 28 g, Fat: 18 g, Carbs: 12 g

Mediterranean Chickpea & Spinach Stew

 Prep Time: 5 minutes *Cook Time: 15 minutes* *Total Time: 20 minutes* *Yield: 2 servings*

  Ingredients

- 1 can (15 oz) chickpeas, drained and rinsed
- 2 cups fresh spinach
- 1 cup diced tomatoes (canned or fresh)
- 1 clove garlic, minced
- 1 tbsp olive oil
- ½ tsp ground cumin
- Salt and pepper, to taste

Instructions

1. **Heat Oil:** In a large skillet or pot, heat olive oil over medium heat until shimmering, about 1 minute.
2. **Cook Garlic:** Add minced garlic to the skillet and sauté until fragrant, about 30 seconds.
3. **Add Tomatoes and Chickpeas:** Add the diced tomatoes and chickpeas to the skillet, stirring to combine. Season with cumin, salt, and pepper. Cook for 5-7 minutes until the tomatoes break down and the mixture thickens slightly.
4. **Add Spinach:** Stir in the spinach and cook for 2-3 minutes, until wilted.
5. **Serve:** Divide the stew between bowls and enjoy warm.

Nutritional Breakdown (Estimated per serving)

Calories: 320 kcal, Protein: 18 g, Fat: 16 g, Carbs: 14 g

Lemon Garlic Chicken Thighs with Roasted Vegetables

 Prep Time: 5 minutes *Cook Time: 20 minutes* *Total Time: 25 minutes*

 Yield: 2 servings

Ingredients

- 2 chicken thighs, bone-in, skin-on
- 1 tbsp olive oil
- 1 tbsp lemon juice
- 1 clove garlic, minced
- 1 cup baby carrots
- 1 cup broccoli florets
- Salt and pepper, to taste

Instructions

1. **Preheat Oven:** Preheat your oven to 400°F (200°C).
2. **Prepare Chicken Thighs:** In a small bowl, mix olive oil, lemon juice, garlic, salt, and pepper. Rub the mixture onto the chicken thighs.
3. **Arrange on Baking Sheet:** Place chicken thighs, baby carrots, and broccoli on a baking sheet. Drizzle a little more olive oil over the vegetables, and season with salt and pepper.
4. **Roast:** Bake for 20 minutes or until the chicken reaches an internal temperature of 165°F and the vegetables are tender.
5. **Serve:** Plate the chicken with the roasted vegetables and enjoy.

Nutritional Breakdown (Estimated per serving)

Calories: 360 kcal, Protein: 28 g, Fat: 18 g, Carbs: 18 g

Beef & Mushroom Stir-Fry

 Prep Time: 5 minutes *Cook Time: 15 minutes* *Total Time: 20 minutes*

 Yield: 2 servings

Ingredients

- 1 cup thinly sliced beef (such as sirloin)
- 1 cup mushrooms, sliced
- 1 tbsp soy sauce
- 1 tbsp olive oil
- 1 clove garlic, minced
- Salt and pepper, to taste

Instructions

1. **Heat Oil:** Warm olive oil in a skillet over medium heat until shimmering, about 1 minute.
2. **Cook Beef:** Add sliced beef to the skillet, season with salt and pepper, and cook until browned, about 5 minutes. Remove beef from the skillet and set aside.
3. **Cook Mushrooms and Garlic:** In the same skillet, add garlic and mushrooms. Sauté until the mushrooms are tender, about 5 minutes.
4. **Combine with Beef:** Return the beef to the skillet, add soy sauce, and stir until well coated.
5. **Serve:** Divide between plates and serve warm.

Nutritional Breakdown (Estimated per serving)

Calories: 340 kcal, Protein: 26 g, Fat: 14 g, Carbs: 14 g

Zesty Shrimp & Cauliflower Rice

 Prep Time: 5 minutes *Cook Time: 10 minutes* *Total Time: 15 minutes*

 Yield: 2 servings

Ingredients

- 1 cup large shrimp, peeled and deveined
- 1 cup cauliflower rice
- 1 tbsp olive oil
- 1 tbsp lime juice
- Salt and pepper, to taste

Instructions

1. **Heat Oil:** In a large skillet, add olive oil and heat over medium until shimmering.
2. **Cook Shrimp:** Add shrimp, season with salt, pepper, and lime juice, and cook for 2-3 minutes on each side until pink and opaque. Remove and set aside.
3. **Add Cauliflower Rice:** In the same skillet, add cauliflower rice and cook for 3-4 minutes until tender.
4. **Serve:** Plate the cauliflower rice and top with shrimp. Serve warm.

Nutritional Breakdown (Estimated per serving)
Calories: 260 kcal, Protein: 22 g, Fat: 10 g, Carbs: 12 g

Honey Mustard Pork Chops & Brussels Sprouts

 Prep Time: 5 minutes *Cook Time: 15 minutes* *Total Time: 20 minutes*

 Yield: 2 servings

Ingredients

- 2 boneless pork chops
- 1 tbsp honey
- 1 tbsp Dijon mustard
- 1 cup Brussels sprouts, halved
- 1 tbsp olive oil
- Salt and pepper, to taste

Instructions

1. **Prepare Sauce:** In a small bowl, mix honey and Dijon mustard until smooth.
2. **Heat Oil:** In a skillet over medium heat, warm olive oil until it shimmers. 3.
3. **Cook Pork Chops:** Season pork chops with salt and pepper. Add them to the skillet and cook for 4-5 minutes per side until golden and cooked through. Remove and brush with honey mustard sauce.
4. **Cook Brussels Sprouts:** In the same skillet, add Brussels sprouts and cook for 5-6 minutes, stirring occasionally, until tender and caramelized.
5. **Serve:** Plate the pork chops and Brussels sprouts together and serve warm.

Nutritional Breakdown (Estimated per serving)
Calories: 360 kcal, Protein: 28 g, Fat: 16 g, Carbs: 16 g

Spaghetti Squash Marinara with Ground Turkey

 Prep Time: 5 minutes *Cook Time: 15 minutes* *Total Time: 20 minutes*

 Yield: 2 servings

Ingredients

- 1 cup cooked spaghetti squash
- 1 cup ground turkey
- 1 cup marinara sauce
- 1 tbsp olive oil
- Salt and pepper, to taste

Instructions

1. **Heat Oil:** In a skillet, add olive oil and heat over medium.
2. **Cook Turkey:** Add ground turkey, season with salt and pepper, and cook until browned, about 8-10 minutes.
3. **Add Marinara Sauce:** Pour marinara sauce over the turkey and stir to combine. Cook for an additional 2-3 minutes until heated through.
4. **Serve:** Divide cooked spaghetti squash between plates and top with the turkey marinara mixture.

Nutritional Breakdown (Estimated per serving)

Calories: 310 kcal, Protein: 22 g, Fat: 12 g, Carbs: 24 g

Thai Basil Chicken Stir-Fry

 Prep Time: 5 minutes *Cook Time: 15 minutes* *Total Time: 20 minutes*

 *Yield: 2 servings*

Ingredients

- 2 chicken breasts, thinly sliced
- 1 tbsp olive oil
- 1 tbsp soy sauce
- 1 tsp fish sauce (optional)
- 1 cup fresh basil leaves
- Salt and pepper, to taste

Instructions

1. **Heat Oil:** Warm olive oil in a skillet over medium heat until shimmering.
2. **Cook Chicken:** Add sliced chicken, season with salt and pepper, and cook until no longer pink, about 7-8 minutes.
3. **Add Sauces and Basil:** Stir in soy sauce, fish sauce, and basil leaves. Cook for an additional 2-3 minutes until basil is wilted.
4. **Serve:** Divide between plates and enjoy warm.

Nutritional Breakdown (Estimated per serving)

Calories: 330 kcal, Protein: 26 g, Fat: 14 g, Carbs: 12 g

Garlic Lemon Cod with Steamed Vegetables

 Prep Time: 5 minutes *Cook Time: 10 minutes* *Total Time: 15 minutes*
 Yield: 2 servings

Ingredients

- 2 cod fillets (4 oz each)
- 1 tbsp olive oil
- 1 clove garlic, minced
- 1 tbsp lemon juice
- 1 cup mixed vegetables (carrots, broccoli)

Instructions

1. **Steam Vegetables:** In a steamer or microwave-safe dish, steam the vegetables until tender, about 5 minutes.
2. **Heat Oil:** In a skillet, warm olive oil over medium heat.
3. **Cook Cod:** Add minced garlic and cod fillets. Season with salt, pepper, and lemon juice. Cook for 3-4 minutes on each side until the fish flakes easily.
4. **Serve:** Plate the cod with steamed vegetables.

> *Nutritional Breakdown (Estimated per serving)*
> Calories: 250 kcal, Protein: 24 g, Fat: 10 g, Carbs: 10 g

Chicken & Veggie Sheet Pan Dinner

 Prep Time: 5 minutes *Cook Time: 20 minutes* *Total Time: 25 minutes*
 Yield: 2 servings

Ingredients

- 2 chicken breasts
- 1 cup mixed vegetables (e.g., bell peppers, zucchini)
- 1 tbsp olive oil
- Salt, pepper, and dried herbs (like thyme or rosemary)

Instructions

1. **Preheat Oven:** Preheat oven to 400°F (200°C).
2. **Prepare Ingredients:** Place the chicken breasts and mixed vegetables on a baking sheet. Drizzle with olive oil, then season with salt, pepper, and a sprinkle of dried herbs like thyme or rosemary. Toss the vegetables to coat evenly.
3. **Bake:** Roast in the preheated oven for 20 minutes, or until the chicken reaches an internal temperature of 165°F (74°C) and the vegetables are tender.
4. **Serve:** Plate the chicken alongside the roasted vegetables and serve immediately

> *Nutritional Breakdown (Estimated per serving)*
> Calories: 300 kcal, Protein: 28 g, Fat: 12 g, Carbs: 18 g

Ginger Soy Beef & Bok Choy Stir-Fry

 Prep Time: 5 minutes *Cook Time: 15 minutes* *Total Time: 20 minutes*

Yield: 2 servings

Ingredients

- 1 cup thinly sliced beef (such as flank or sirloin)
- 2 cups bok choy, chopped
- 1 tbsp soy sauce
- 1 tsp grated ginger
- 1 tbsp olive oil

Instructions

1. **Heat Oil:** In a large skillet or wok, heat the olive oil over medium heat until it shimmers, about 1 minute.
2. **Cook Beef:** Add the beef slices to the skillet, season with salt and pepper, and cook until browned, about 5-6 minutes. Remove beef from the skillet and set aside.
3. **Add Bok Choy and Ginger:** In the same skillet, add the chopped bok choy and grated ginger. Sauté, stirring frequently, until the bok choy is tender, about 3-4 minutes.
4. **Combine and Season:** Return the beef to the skillet, add soy sauce, and toss to coat evenly. Cook for an additional 2 minutes to heat through.
5. **Serve:** Divide between plates and enjoy warm.

Nutritional Breakdown (Estimated per serving)
Calories: 330 kcal, Protein: 24 g, Fat: 14 g, Carbs: 12 g

Herbed Turkey Meatballs with Zucchini Noodles

 Prep Time: 5 minutes *Cook Time: 15 minutes* *Total Time: 20 minutes*

Yield: 2 servings

Ingredients

- ½ lb ground turkey
- 1 tbsp chopped fresh parsley
- 1 clove garlic, minced
- 1 cup zucchini noodles (zoodles)
- 1 tbsp olive oil
- Salt and pepper, to taste

Instructions

1. **Prepare Meatballs:** In a mixing bowl, combine ground turkey, parsley, garlic, salt, and pepper. Form the mixture into small meatballs, about 1 inch in diameter.
2. **Cook Meatballs:** In a skillet, heat olive oil over medium heat. Add the meatballs and cook, turning occasionally, until browned on all sides and cooked through, about 10-12 minutes.
3. **Add Zoodles:** Add the zucchini noodles to the skillet and cook for 1-2 minutes, tossing gently, until just softened.
4. **Serve:** Divide the meatballs and zoodles between plates. Serve warm.

Nutritional Breakdown (Estimated per serving)
Calories: 340 kcal, Protein: 28 g, Fat: 14 g, Carbs: 10 g

Lemon Thyme Roast Chicken Thighs

 Prep Time: 5 minutes *Cook Time: 20 minutes* *Total Time: 25 minutes*

 Yield: 2 servings

Ingredients

- 4 bone-in, skin-on chicken thighs
- 1 tbsp olive oil
- 1 tbsp lemon juice
- 1 tsp fresh thyme leaves
- Salt and pepper, to taste

Instructions

1. **Preheat Oven:** Preheat your oven to 400°F (200°C).
2. **Prepare Chicken:** In a small bowl, mix olive oil, lemon juice, thyme, salt, and pepper. Rub the mixture onto each chicken thigh, coating evenly.
3. **Roast:** Arrange chicken thighs on a baking sheet and roast in the oven for 20 minutes, or until the internal temperature reaches 165°F (74°C).
4. **Serve:** Plate the chicken and drizzle any pan juices over the top. Serve immediately.

Nutritional Breakdown (Estimated per serving)
Calories: 320 kcal, Protein: 26 g, Fat: 18 g, Carbs: 6 g

Honey Mustard Chicken Breast with Green Beans

 Prep Time: 5 minutes *Cook Time: 15 minutes* *Total Time: 20 minutes*

 Yield: 2 servings

Ingredients

- 2 boneless, skinless chicken breasts
- 1 tbsp honey
- 1 tbsp Dijon mustard
- 1 tbsp olive oil
- 1 cup green beans, trimmed
- Salt and pepper, to taste

Instructions

1. **Heat Oil:** In a skillet, warm olive oil over medium heat until shimmering, about 1 minute.
2. **Prepare Sauce:** In a small bowl, mix honey and Dijon mustard until smooth. Set aside.
3. **Cook Chicken:** Add the chicken breasts to the skillet and season with salt and pepper. Cook for 5-6 minutes per side until golden brown and fully cooked. Remove from skillet and brush with honey mustard sauce.
4. **Cook Green Beans:** Add green beans to the skillet, sautéing until tender, about 4-5 minutes.
5. **Serve:** Plate the chicken with green beans and serve immediately.

Nutritional Breakdown (Estimated per serving)
Calories: 290 kcal, Protein: 28 g, Fat: 10 g, Carbs: 16 g

Garlic Rosemary Chicken Drumsticks

 Prep Time: 5 minutes *Cook Time: 20 minutes* *Total Time: 25 minutes*

 Yield: 2 servings

Ingredients

- 4 chicken drumsticks
- 1 tbsp olive oil
- 1 clove garlic, minced
- 1 tsp fresh rosemary, chopped
- Salt and pepper, to taste

Instructions

1. **Preheat Oven:** Preheat oven to 425°F (220°C).
2. **Season Chicken:** In a small bowl, mix olive oil, garlic, rosemary, salt, and pepper. Rub the mixture onto the drumsticks.
3. **Bake:** Place drumsticks on a baking sheet and bake for 20-25 minutes, or until the internal temperature reaches 165°F (74°C).
4. **Serve:** Remove from the oven and serve warm.

Nutritional Breakdown (Estimated per serving)
Calories: 310 kcal, Protein: 24 g, Fat: 16 g, Carbs: 6 g

Herbed Turkey Cutlets with Spinach

 Prep Time: 5 minutes *Cook Time: 10 minutes* *Total Time: 15 minutes*

Yield: 2 servings

Ingredients

- 2 turkey cutlets
- 1 tbsp olive oil
- 1 tsp dried Italian herbs
- 2 cups spinach
- Salt and pepper, to taste

Instructions

1. **Heat Oil:** In a large skillet, warm olive oil over medium heat.
2. **Cook Turkey:** Season turkey cutlets with Italian herbs, salt, and pepper. Add to the skillet and cook for 3-4 minutes per side until golden and fully cooked. Remove and set aside.
3. **Cook Spinach:** In the same skillet, add spinach and sauté until wilted, about 2 minutes.
4. **Serve:** Plate the turkey cutlets with spinach and serve immediately.

Nutritional Breakdown (Estimated per serving)
Calories: 260 kcal, Protein: 26 g, Fat: 14 g, Carbs: 6 g

Maple Glazed Chicken Tenders

 Prep Time: 5 minutes *Cook Time: 10 minutes* *Total Time: 15 minutes*

Yield: 2 servings

Ingredients

- 1 cup chicken tenders
- 1 tbsp maple syrup
- 1 tbsp olive oil
- ½ tsp paprika
- Salt and pepper, to taste

Instructions

1. Heat Oil: In a skillet over medium heat, add olive oil and warm until shimmering, about 1 minute.

2. Cook Chicken: Add chicken tenders to the skillet, season with paprika, salt, and pepper, and cook for 3-4 minutes per side until golden and cooked through.

3. Add Maple Syrup: Drizzle maple syrup over the chicken and cook for an additional minute, tossing to coat.

4. Serve: Plate the chicken and serve immediately.

Nutritional Breakdown (Estimated per serving)
Calories: 300 kcal, Protein: 24 g, Fat: 10 g, Carbs: 18 g

Balsamic Glazed Chicken Breast with Mushrooms

 Prep Time: 5 minutes *Cook Time: 15 minutes* *Total Time: 20 minutes*

Yield: 2 servings

Ingredients

- 2 chicken breasts
- 1 cup sliced mushrooms
- 1 tbsp balsamic vinegar
- 1 tbsp olive oil
- Salt and pepper, to taste

Instructions

1. Heat Oil: In a skillet, add olive oil and warm over medium heat.

2. Cook Chicken: Season chicken breasts with salt and pepper. Place in the skillet and cook for 5-6 minutes per side until golden and fully cooked. Remove from skillet and set aside.

3. Cook Mushrooms and Add Balsamic: Add mushrooms to the skillet and cook for 3-4 minutes until tender. Drizzle balsamic vinegar over the mushrooms, stirring to coat.

4. Serve: Plate the chicken with the balsamic mushrooms on the side.

Nutritional Breakdown (Estimated per serving)
Calories: 320 kcal, Protein: 26 g, Fat: 12 g, Carbs: 14 g

Orange Ginger Glazed Duck Breast

 Prep Time: 5 minutes *Cook Time: 20 minutes* *Total Time: 25 minutes*
 Yield: 2 servings

Ingredients

- 1 duck breast
- 1 tbsp orange juice
- ½ tsp grated ginger
- Salt and pepper, to taste

Instructions

1. **Preheat Oven:** Preheat oven to 400°F (200°C).
2. **Score Duck Skin:** Lightly score the skin of the duck breast with a sharp knife. Season with salt and pepper.
3. **Cook Duck:** In a skillet over medium heat, place the duck breast skin-side down and cook for 6-7 minutes until crispy. Flip and cook the other side for 2 minutes.
4. **Glaze:** Remove duck from heat and brush with orange juice and grated ginger. Transfer to oven and roast for an additional 8-10 minutes until cooked to your preference.
5. **Serve:** Slice and serve warm.

Nutritional Breakdown (Estimated per serving)

Calories: 350 kcal, Protein: 24 g, Fat: 18 g, Carbs: 16 g

Teriyaki Chicken Thighs with Bell Peppers

 Prep Time: 5 minutes *Cook Time: 15minutes* *Total Time: 20 minutes*
Yield: 2 servings

Ingredients

- 4 chicken thighs
- 1 tbsp teriyaki sauce
- 1 cup bell peppers, sliced
- 1 tbsp olive oil

Instructions

1. **Heat Oil:** In a large skillet, warm olive oil over medium heat.
2. **Cook Chicken Thighs:** Add the chicken thighs and cook for 5-6 minutes per side until golden and cooked through.
3. **Add Bell Peppers and Teriyaki Sauce:** Add bell peppers and teriyaki sauce to the skillet. Toss to coat and cook for 3-4 minutes until peppers are tender.
4. **Serve:** Plate the chicken with bell peppers and serve warm.

Nutritional Breakdown (Estimated per serving)
Calories: 340 kcal, Protein: 26 g, Fat: 14 g, Carbs: 18 g

CHAPTER 6: BEEF, LAMB, AND PORK

Herb-Crusted Lamb Chops with Garlic Spinach

 Prep Time: 5 minutes Cook Time: 15 minutes Total Time: 20 minutes
Yield: 2 servings

Ingredients

- 4 small lamb chops
- 1 tbsp fresh rosemary, chopped
- 1 tbsp fresh thyme, chopped
- 1 clove garlic, minced
- 1 tbsp olive oil
- 2 cups fresh spinach
- Salt and pepper, to taste

Instructions

1. **Season Lamb Chops:** In a small bowl, mix rosemary, thyme, garlic, salt, and pepper. Rub the herb mixture onto both sides of the lamb chops.
2. **Cook Lamb:** Heat 1 tbsp of olive oil in a skillet over medium-high heat. Add lamb chops and cook for 3-4 minutes on each side, until they reach your desired doneness. Remove from skillet and set aside.
3. **Sauté Spinach:** In the same skillet, add spinach and sauté for 1-2 minutes until wilted. Season with a pinch of salt.
4. **Serve:** Plate lamb chops alongside the garlic spinach and serve warm.

Nutritional Breakdown (Estimated per serving)
Calories: 360 kcal, Protein: 26 g, Fat: 24 g, Carbs: 8 g

Garlic Butter Ribeye with Asparagus

 Prep Time: 5 minutes Cook Time: 10 minutes Total Time: 15 minutes
Yield: 2 servings

Ingredients

- 1 ribeye steak (8 oz)
- 1 tbsp butter
- 1 clove garlic, minced
- 1 cup asparagus spears, trimmed
- Salt and pepper, to taste

Instructions

1. **Season Steak:** Season the ribeye with salt and pepper on both sides.
2. **Cook Steak:** Heat a skillet over medium-high heat and add the butter. Once melted, add the ribeye and cook for 3-4 minutes on each side, depending on desired doneness. Add garlic in the last minute of cooking for added flavor. Remove steak from the skillet and let it rest.
3. **Cook Asparagus:** In the same skillet, add asparagus and cook for 3-4 minutes until tender-crisp.
4. **Serve:** Slice the steak and serve with the asparagus on the side.

Nutritional Breakdown (Estimated per serving)
Calories: 400 kcal, Protein: 28 g, Fat: 28 g, Carbs: 6 g

Rosemary & Honey Glazed Pork Tenderloin

 Prep Time: 5 minutes *Cook Time: 20 minutes* *Total Time: 25 minutes*
Yield: 2 servings

Ingredients

- 1 pork tenderloin (8 oz)
- 1 tbsp honey
- 1 tsp fresh rosemary, chopped
- 1 tbsp olive oil
- Salt and pepper, to taste

Instructions

1. **Preheat Oven:** Preheat oven to 400°F (200°C).
2. **Season Pork:** Rub the pork tenderloin with olive oil, rosemary, salt, and pepper. Drizzle honey on top.
3. **Sear Pork:** In a skillet over medium heat, sear the pork tenderloin for 2-3 minutes on each side.
4. **Roast:** Transfer the pork to the oven and roast for 15-18 minutes until it reaches an internal temperature of 145°F (63°C).
5. **Serve:** Let the pork rest for a few minutes, then slice and serve warm.

Nutritional Breakdown (Estimated per serving)
Calories: 340 kcal, Protein: 26 g, Fat: 10 g, Carbs: 28 g

Seared Lamb Cutlets with Mint Yogurt Sauce

 Prep Time: 5 minutes *Cook Time: 10 minutes* *Total Time: 15 minutes*
 Yield: 2 servings

Ingredients

- 4 lamb cutlets
- 1 tbsp olive oil
- Salt and pepper, to taste
- ¼ cup Greek yogurt
- 1 tbsp fresh mint, chopped

Instructions

1. **Season Lamb:** Season lamb cutlets with salt and pepper.
2. **Cook Lamb:** In a skillet over medium-high heat, add olive oil. Sear the lamb cutlets for 3-4 minutes on each side for medium-rare. Remove from skillet and let rest.
3. **Prepare Sauce:** In a small bowl, mix Greek yogurt and chopped mint.
4. **Serve:** Plate lamb cutlets with a spoonful of mint yogurt sauce.

Nutritional Breakdown (Estimated per serving)
Calories: 330 kcal, Protein: 26 g, Fat: 18 g, Carbs: 10 g

Mustard Crusted Pork Chops with Brussels Sprouts

 Prep Time: 5 minutes Cook Time: 15 minutes Total Time: 20 minutes

 Yield: 2 servings

Ingredients

- 2 pork chops
- 1 tbsp Dijon mustard
- 1 tbsp olive oil
- 1 cup Brussels sprouts, halved
- Salt and pepper, to taste

Instructions

1. **Season and Coat Pork:** Brush pork chops with Dijon mustard and season with salt and pepper.
2. **Cook Pork:** Heat olive oil in a skillet over medium-high heat. Add pork chops and cook for 4-5 minutes on each side until golden and cooked through. Remove and set aside.
3. **Cook Brussels Sprouts:** In the same skillet, add Brussels sprouts and cook until tender, about 5-6 minutes.
4. **Serve:** Plate pork chops with Brussels sprouts.

Nutritional Breakdown (Estimated per serving)
Calories: 320 kcal, Protein: 26 g, Fat: 18 g, Carbs: 12 g

Ground Beef & Zucchini Stir-Fry

 Prep Time: 5 minutes Cook Time: 10 minutes Total Time: 15 minutes

Yield: 2 servings

Ingredients

- 1 cup ground beef
- 1 cup zucchini, diced
- 1 tbsp soy sauce
- 1 tbsp olive oil
- Salt and pepper, to taste

Instructions

1. **Cook Beef:** In a skillet over medium heat, add ground beef, season with salt and pepper, and cook until browned, about 5 minutes.
2. **Add Zucchini and Soy Sauce:** Add diced zucchini and soy sauce to the skillet. Cook for an additional 3-4 minutes until the zucchini is tender.
3. **Serve:** Divide between plates and enjoy warm.

Nutritional Breakdown (Estimated per serving)
Calories: 290 kcal, Protein: 24 g, Fat: 16 g, Carbs: 8 g

Spiced Lamb Meatballs with Tomato Sauce

 Prep Time: 5 minutes *Cook Time: 15 minutes* *Total Time: 20 minutes*

Yield: 2 servings

Ingredients

- ½ lb ground lamb
- 1 tsp cumin
- 1 tsp paprika
- 1 cup tomato sauce
- 1 tbsp olive oil
- Salt and pepper, to taste

Instructions

1. **Prepare Meatballs:** In a bowl, mix ground lamb, cumin, paprika, salt, and pepper. Form into small meatballs.
2. **Cook Meatballs:** In a skillet, heat olive oil over medium heat. Add meatballs and cook for 8-10 minutes until browned on all sides.
3. **Add Tomato Sauce:** Pour tomato sauce over the meatballs, reduce heat, and simmer for 5 minutes.
4. **Serve:** Plate the meatballs with sauce and enjoy.

Nutritional Breakdown (Estimated per serving)
Calories: 350 kcal, Protein: 26 g, Fat: 20 g, Carbs: 10 g

Honey Glazed Pork Belly with Bok Choy

 Prep Time: 5 minutes *Cook Time: 15 minutes* *Total Time: 20 minutes*

Yield: 2 servings

Ingredients

- ½ lb pork belly, sliced
- 1 tbsp honey
- 1 tbsp soy sauce
- 1 cup bok choy, chopped
- Salt and pepper, to taste

Instructions

1. **Cook Pork Belly:** In a skillet over medium-high heat, cook pork belly slices until crispy, about 5 minutes per side. Remove and set aside.
2. **Add Glaze and Bok Choy:** In the same skillet, add honey, soy sauce, and bok choy. Toss to coat and cook for 2-3 minutes until bok choy is tender.
3. **Add Glaze and Bok Choy:** In the same skillet, add honey and soy sauce. Stir well, then add the chopped bok choy, tossing to coat in the glaze. Cook for 2-3 minutes, stirring occasionally, until the bok choy is tender and slightly wilted.
4. **Serve:** Plate the crispy pork belly with the glazed bok choy and serve immediately.

Nutritional Breakdown (Estimated per serving)
Calories: 420 kcal, Protein: 20 g, Fat: 36 g, Carbs: 12 g

Balsamic Glazed Beef Tenderloin with Mushrooms

 Prep Time: 5 minutes Cook Time: 15 minutes Total Time: 20 minutes
 Yield: 2 servings

Ingredients

- 2 beef tenderloin steaks (4 oz each)
- 1 tbsp balsamic vinegar
- 1 tbsp olive oil
- 1 cup mushrooms, sliced
- Salt and pepper, to taste

Instructions

1. **Heat Oil:** In a skillet, heat olive oil over medium-high heat until it begins to shimmer, about 1 minute.
2. **Cook Steaks:** Season the beef tenderloins with salt and pepper. Place in the skillet and cook for 3-4 minutes on each side, depending on desired doneness. Remove steaks from the skillet and set aside.
3. **Cook Mushrooms and Glaze:** In the same skillet, add sliced mushrooms and cook for 2-3 minutes until they soften. Add balsamic vinegar, stirring to coat the mushrooms in the glaze, and cook for an additional 1-2 minutes.
4. **Serve:** Plate the steaks with mushrooms and drizzle any remaining glaze over the top. Serve warm

---

Nutritional Breakdown (Estimated per serving)
Calories: 370 kcal, Protein: 28 g, Fat: 20 g, Carbs: 10 g

Garlic Herb Lamb Steaks with Mashed Cauliflower

 Prep Time: 5 minutes Cook Time: 15 minutes Total Time: 20 minutes
 Yield: 2 servings

Ingredients

- 2 lamb steaks
- 1 tbsp olive oil
- 1 clove garlic, minced
- 1 tsp fresh rosemary, chopped
- 1 cup cauliflower, steamed and mashed
- Salt and pepper, to taste

Instructions

1. **Season Lamb Steaks:** Rub lamb steaks with olive oil, garlic, rosemary, salt, and pepper.
2. **Cook Lamb:** Heat a skillet over medium-high heat. Add the lamb steaks and cook for 4-5 minutes per side until they reach your desired doneness. Remove from skillet and let rest.
3. **Prepare Cauliflower Mash:** In the same skillet, add the mashed cauliflower and season with a pinch of salt and pepper. Stir until heated through, about 1-2 minutes.
4. **Serve:** Plate the lamb steaks with a side of mashed cauliflower and serve warm.

Nutritional Breakdown (Estimated per serving)
Calories: 380 kcal, Protein: 28 g, Fat: 22 g, Carbs: 12 g

CHAPTER 7: FISH AND SEAFOOD

Lemon Herb Salmon with Asparagus

 Prep Time: 5 minutes Cook Time: 10 minutes Total Time: 15 minutes

Yield: 2 servings

Ingredients

- 2 salmon fillets (4 oz each)
- 1 tbsp olive oil
- 1 tbsp lemon juice
- 1 tsp fresh dill, chopped
- 1 cup asparagus, trimmed
- Salt and pepper, to taste

Instructions

1. **Season Salmon:** Rub salmon fillets with olive oil, lemon juice, dill, salt, and pepper.
2. **Cook Salmon:** In a skillet over medium heat, cook the salmon skin-side down for 4-5 minutes per side until it flakes easily with a fork. Remove and set aside.
3. **Sauté Asparagus:** In the same skillet, add asparagus and cook for 3-4 minutes until tender-crisp.
4. **Serve:** Plate the salmon with asparagus on the side.

Nutritional Breakdown (Estimated per serving)
Calories: 280 kcal, Protein: 24 g, Fat: 16 g, Carbs: 8 g

Garlic Butter Shrimp & Zoodles

 Prep Time: 5 minutes Cook Time: 10 minutes Total Time: 15 minutes

Yield: 2 servings

Ingredients

- 1 cup large shrimp, peeled and deveined
- 2 cups zucchini noodles
- 1 tbsp butter
- 1 clove garlic, minced
- Salt and pepper, to taste

Instructions

1. **Cook Shrimp:** Melt butter in a skillet over medium heat. Add garlic and shrimp, season with salt and pepper, and cook for 2-3 minutes per side until pink and opaque. Remove shrimp and set aside.
2. **Sauté Zoodles:** In the same skillet, add zucchini noodles and cook for 2-3 minutes until just softened.
3. **Serve:** Plate the zoodles and top with cooked shrimp

Nutritional Breakdown (Estimated per serving)
Calories: 260 kcal, Protein: 18 g, Fat: 14 g, Carbs: 10 g

Coconut Curry Cod

 Prep Time: 5 minutes *Cook Time: 15 minutes* *Total Time: 20 minutes*

 Yield: 2 servings

Ingredients

- 2 cod fillets (4 oz each)
- 1 cup coconut milk
- 1 tbsp curry powder
- 1 tbsp olive oil
- Salt and pepper, to taste

Instructions

1. Season Cod: Rub cod fillets with curry powder, salt, and pepper.
2. Cook Cod: In a skillet over medium heat, warm olive oil and cook cod for 3-4 minutes on each side until cooked through.
3. Add Coconut Milk: Pour in coconut milk and simmer for 2-3 minutes until sauce thickens.
4. Serve: Plate the cod with the coconut curry sauce.

> *Nutritional Breakdown (Estimated per serving)*
> Calories: 300 kcal, Protein: 20 g, Fat: 18 g, Carbs: 10 g

Lemon Garlic Tilapia with Spinach

 Prep Time: 5 minutes 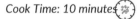 *Cook Time: 10 minutes* *Total Time: 15 minutes*

 Yield: 2 servings

Ingredients

- 2 tilapia fillets
- 1 tbsp olive oil
- 1 tbsp lemon juice
- 2 cups spinach
- Salt and pepper, to taste

Instructions

1. **Season Tilapia:** Rub tilapia fillets with lemon juice, salt, and pepper.
2. **Cook Tilapia:** Heat olive oil in a skillet over medium heat. Add tilapia and cook for 3-4 minutes per side until golden and flaky. Remove and set aside.
3. **Sauté Spinach:** In the same skillet, add spinach and cook until wilted, about 2 minutes.
4. **Serve:** Plate the tilapia with spinach on the side.

> *Nutritional Breakdown (Estimated per serving)*
> Calories: 220 kcal, Protein: 20 g, Fat: 12 g, Carbs: 6 g

Chili Lime Grilled Shrimp

 Prep Time: 5 minutes *Cook Time: 5 minutes* *Total Time: 10 minutes*  *Yield: 2 servings*

Ingredients

- 1 cup large shrimp, peeled and deveined
- 1 tbsp olive oil
- 1 tbsp lime juice
- ½ tsp chili powder
- Salt and pepper, to taste

Instructions

1. Marinate Shrimp: In a bowl, toss shrimp with olive oil, lime juice, chili powder, salt, and pepper.

2. Grill Shrimp: Preheat a grill or skillet over medium-high heat. Grill shrimp for 2-3 minutes per side until pink and cooked through.

3. Serve: Plate and serve warm.

Nutritional Breakdown (Estimated per serving)
Calories: 180 kcal, Protein: 18 g, Fat: 8 g, Carbs: 6 g

Baked Lemon Pepper Trout

 Prep Time: 5 minutes *Cook Time: 15 minutes* *Total Time: 20 minutes* *Yield: 2 servings*

Ingredients

- 2 trout fillets
- 1 tbsp olive oil
- 1 tbsp lemon juice
- ½ tsp black pepper
- Salt, to taste

Instructions

1. **Preheat Oven:** Preheat oven to 400°F (200°C).
2. **Season Trout:** Place trout fillets on a baking sheet. Drizzle with olive oil, lemon juice, black pepper, and salt.
3. **Bake:** Bake for 12-15 minutes until the trout is flaky and opaque.
4. **Serve:** Plate and serve immediately.

Nutritional Breakdown (Estimated per serving)
Calories: 250 kcal, Protein: 24 g, Fat: 14 g, Carbs: 4 g

Thai Basil Shrimp Stir-Fry

Ingredients

- 1 cup shrimp, peeled and deveined
- 1 tbsp soy sauce
- 1 tbsp fresh basil, chopped
- 1 tbsp olive oil
- Salt and pepper, to taste

 Prep Time: 5 minutes Cook Time: 10 minutes Total Time: 15 minutes

 Yield: 2 servings

Instructions

1. **Cook Shrimp:** In a skillet over medium heat, add olive oil and shrimp. Season with salt and pepper, and cook for 2-3 minutes per side until pink.
2. **Add Soy Sauce and Basil:** Add soy sauce and fresh basil, tossing to coat. Cook for 1 more minute.
3. **Serve:** Plate and serve immediately.

Nutritional Breakdown (Estimated per serving)
Calories: 220 kcal, Protein: 20 g, Fat: 12 g, Carbs: 6 g

Herb-Crusted Tuna Steak

Ingredients

- 2 tuna steaks (4 oz each)
- 1 tbsp olive oil
- 1 tsp dried herbs (thyme, rosemary)
- Salt and pepper, to taste

 Prep Time: 5 minutes Cook Time: 6 minutes Total Time: 11 minutes

 Yield: 2 servings

Instructions

1. **Season Tuna:** Rub tuna steaks with olive oil, herbs, salt, and pepper.
2. **Cook Tuna:** Heat a skillet over medium-high heat. Add tuna and sear for 2-3 minutes per side for medium-rare.
3. **Serve:** Slice and serve immediately.

Nutritional Breakdown (Estimated per serving)
Calories: 300 kcal, Protein: 28 g, Fat: 16 g, Carbs: 4 g

Parmesan Crusted Halibut

 Prep Time: 5 minutes *Cook Time: 10 minutes* *Total Time: 15 minutes*

 Yield: 2 servings

Ingredients

- 2 halibut fillets
- 2 tbsp grated Parmesan cheese
- 1 tbsp olive oil
- Salt and pepper, to taste

Instructions

1. **Coat Halibut:** Pat the halibut fillets dry and sprinkle with salt, pepper, and Parmesan.
2. **Cook Halibut:** In a skillet over medium heat, add olive oil. Place halibut in the skillet and cook for 4-5 minutes per side until golden and cooked through.
3. **Serve:** Plate and serve immediately.

Nutritional Breakdown (Estimated per serving)
Calories: 280 kcal, Protein: 24 g, Fat: 14 g, Carbs: 6 g

Sesame Crusted Seared Tuna

 Prep Time: 5 minutes *Cook Time: 6 minutes* *Total Time: 11 minutes*

 Yield: 2 servings

Ingredients

- 2 tuna steaks (4 oz each)
- 1 tbsp sesame oil
- 2 tbsp sesame seeds (white or black)
- Salt and pepper, to taste

Instructions

1. **Season and Coat Tuna:** Pat the tuna steaks dry, season with salt and pepper, and press sesame seeds onto both sides of each steak to create an even crust.
2. **Heat Oil:** In a skillet over medium-high heat, add sesame oil and warm until shimmering.
3. **Sear Tuna:** Place the tuna steaks in the skillet and cook for 2-3 minutes per side for a medium-rare finish. Adjust time for preferred doneness.
4. **Serve:** Slice the tuna steaks thinly and serve immediately.

Nutritional Breakdown (Estimated per serving)
Calories: 320 kcal, Protein: 28 g, Fat: 18 g, Carbs: 4 g

CHAPTER 8: SOUPS AND STEWS

Creamy Coconut Chicken Soup

 Prep Time: 5 minutes Cook Time: 15minutes Total Time: 20 minutes

Yield: 2 servings

Ingredients

- 1 cup diced chicken breast
- 1 cup coconut milk
- 1 cup chicken broth
- ½ cup sliced mushrooms
- 1 tbsp fresh ginger, grated
- 1 tbsp olive oil
- Salt and pepper, to taste

Instructions

1. **Heat Oil:** In a pot over medium heat, warm the olive oil until shimmering, about 1 minute.
2. **Cook Chicken and Mushrooms:** Add the diced chicken and mushrooms, season with salt and pepper, and cook until chicken is browned, about 5 minutes.
3. **Add Broth and Coconut Milk:** Pour in chicken broth, coconut milk, and grated ginger. Stir to combine.
4. **Simmer:** Reduce heat and simmer for 10 minutes until the soup is heated through.
5. **Serve:** Ladle into bowls and serve warm.

Nutritional Breakdown (Estimated per serving)
Calories: 280 kcal, Protein: 20 g, Fat: 16 g, Carbs: 12 g

Beef and Vegetable Stew

 Prep Time: 5 minutes Cook Time: 20 minutes Total Time: 25 minutes

Yield: 2 servings

Ingredients

- 1 cup diced beef 1 cup
- beef broth ½ cup
- carrots, diced ½ cup
- potatoes, diced ½ cup
- onions, chopped 1 tbsp
- olive oil Salt and pepper,
- to taste

Instructions

1. **Heat Oil:** In a pot, warm olive oil over medium heat until it shimmers.
2. **Cook Beef and Onions:** Add the beef and onions, season with salt and pepper, and cook until browned, about 5 minutes.
3. **Add Vegetables and Broth:** Add carrots, potatoes, and beef broth.
Stir well and bring to a simmer.
4. **Simmer:** Cover and cook for 15 minutes until vegetables are tender.
5. **Serve:** Ladle into bowls and enjoy warm.

Nutritional Breakdown (Estimated per serving)
Calories: 340 kcal, Protein: 26 g, Fat: 18 g, Carbs: 20 g

Spiced Lentil & Spinach Soup

 Prep Time: 5 minutes *Cook Time: 20 minutes* *Total Time: 25 minutes*

 Yield: 2 servings

Ingredients

- 1 cup cooked lentils 2
- cups vegetable broth 1
- cup fresh spinach 1 tsp
- ground cumin 1 tsp
- ground turmeric 1 tbsp
- olive oil Salt and pepper,
- to taste

Instructions

1. **Heat Oil:** In a pot, add olive oil and heat over medium.

2. **Add Spices:** Stir in cumin and turmeric, cooking for 1 minute until fragrant.

3. **Add Lentils and Broth:** Add lentils and vegetable broth, stirring to combine.

4. **Simmer:** Bring to a simmer, cover, and cook for 15 minutes. Stir in spinach and cook until wilted, about 2 minutes.

5. **Serve:** Ladle into bowls and serve warm.

> *Nutritional Breakdown (Estimated per serving)*
> Calories: 250 kcal, Protein: 12 g, Fat: 8 g, Carbs: 28 g

Ginger Carrot Soup

 Prep Time: 5 minutes *Cook Time: 15 minutes* *Total Time: 20 minutes*

Yield: 2 servings

Ingredients

- 2 cups carrots, diced
- 2 cups vegetable broth
- 1 tbsp fresh ginger, grated
- 1 tbsp olive oil
- Salt and pepper, to taste

Instructions

1. **Heat Oil:** In a pot over medium heat, warm olive oil until shimmering.
2. **Cook Carrots and Ginger:** Add carrots and ginger, season with salt and pepper, and cook for 5 minutes.
3. **Add Broth and Simmer:** Pour in the vegetable broth, bring to a simmer, and cook for 15 minutes until carrots are tender.
4. **Blend:** Use an immersion blender to puree the soup until smooth.
5. **Serve:** Ladle into bowls and serve warm.

> *Nutritional Breakdown (Estimated per serving)*
> Calories: 180 kcal, Protein: 4 g, Fat: 6 g, Carbs: 28 g

Creamy Tomato Basil Soup

 Prep Time: 5 minutes *Cook Time: 15 minutes* *Total Time: 20 minutes*

 Yield: 2 servings

Ingredients

- 1 can (15 oz) diced tomatoes
- 1 cup vegetable broth
- ¼ cup coconut milk
- 1 tbsp fresh basil, chopped
- Salt and pepper, to taste

Instructions

1. **Combine Ingredients:** In a pot, add diced tomatoes, vegetable broth, coconut milk, salt, and pepper.
2. **Simmer:** Bring to a simmer over medium heat and cook for 15 minutes.
3. **Blend:** Use an immersion blender to blend until smooth.
4. **Add Basil and Serve:** Stir in basil and serve warm.

> *Nutritional Breakdown (Estimated per serving)*
> Calories: 220 kcal, Protein: 6 g, Fat: 12 g, Carbs: 22 g

Hearty Beef & Barley Soup

 Prep Time: 5 minutes Cook Time: 20 minutes Total Time: 25 minutes

Yield: 2 servings

Ingredients

- 1 cup diced beef
- 2 cups beef broth
- ¼ cup barley
- ½ cup carrots, diced
- Salt and pepper, to taste

Instructions

1. **Cook Beef:** In a pot over medium heat, cook diced beef until browned, about 5 minutes.
2. **Add Barley, Carrots, and Broth:** Add barley, carrots, beef broth, salt, and pepper.
3. **Simmer:** Bring to a simmer, cover, and cook for 20 minutes until barley is tender.
4. **Serve:** Ladle into bowls and enjoy warm.

Nutritional Breakdown (Estimated per serving)
Calories: 330 kcal, Protein: 24 g, Fat: 10 g, Carbs: 38 g

Spicy Sausage & Kale Soup

 Prep Time: 5 minutes Cook Time: 15 minutes Total Time: 20 minutes

Yield: 2 servings

Ingredients

- 1 cup sliced sausage
- 1 cup chopped kale
- 2 cups chicken broth
- 1 tsp red pepper flakes
- Salt and pepper, to taste

Instructions

1. **Cook Sausage:** In a pot over medium heat, cook sliced sausage until browned, about 5 minutes.
2. **Add Kale, Broth, and Spices:** Add kale, chicken broth, red pepper flakes, salt, and pepper.
3. **Simmer:** Bring to a simmer and cook for 10 minutes until kale is tender.
4. **Serve:** Ladle into bowls and serve warm.

Nutritional Breakdown (Estimated per serving)
Calories: 300 kcal, Protein: 18 g, Fat: 18 g, Carbs: 16 g

Turkey & Sweet Potato Stew

Prep Time: 5 minutes Cook Time: 20 minutes Total Time: 25 minutes

Yield: 2 servings

Ingredients

- 1 cup ground turkey
- 1 cup diced sweet potatoes
- 2 cups chicken broth
- 1 tsp dried thyme
- Salt and pepper, to taste

Instructions

1. **Cook Turkey:** In a pot over medium heat, cook the ground turkey until browned, about 5 minutes.
2. **Add Sweet Potatoes and Broth:** Add sweet potatoes, chicken broth, thyme, salt, and pepper.
3. **Simmer:** Bring to a simmer, cover, and cook for 15 minutes until sweet potatoes are tender.
4. **Serve:** Ladle into bowls and enjoy.

Nutritional Breakdown (Estimated per serving)
Calories: 320 kcal, Protein: 24 g, Fat: 10 g, Carbs: 28 g

CHAPTER 9: SALADS

Lemon Herb Grilled Chicken Salad

 Prep Time: 5 minutes Cook Time: 10 minutes Total Time: 15 minutes

Yield: 2 servings

Ingredients

- 1 boneless, skinless chicken breast
- 2 cups mixed greens
- 1 tbsp fresh parsley, chopped
- 1 tbsp fresh basil, chopped
- 1 tbsp olive oil
- 1 tbsp lemon juice
- Salt and pepper, to taste

Instructions

1. Season and Grill Chicken: Season the chicken breast with salt, pepper, and a drizzle of olive oil. Grill over medium heat for 4-5 minutes per side, or until fully cooked. Remove, let rest, and slice thinly.

2. Prepare Dressing: In a small bowl, whisk together olive oil, lemon juice, salt, and pepper.

3. Assemble Salad: In a large bowl, combine mixed greens, parsley, basil, and grilled chicken slices. Drizzle with dressing and toss to coat.

4. Serve: Divide between plates and serve immediately.

Nutritional Breakdown (Estimated per serving)
Calories: 320 kcal, Protein: 24 g, Fat: 14 g, Carbs: 12 g

Pan-Seared Salmon & Arugula Salad

 Prep Time: 5 minutes Cook Time: 10 minutes Total Time: 15 minutes

Yield: 2 servings

Ingredients

- 1 salmon fillet (4 oz)
- 2 cups arugula
- ½ cup cherry tomatoes, halved
- 1 tbsp olive oil
- 1 tbsp lemon juice
- Salt and pepper, to taste

Instructions

1. Season and Sear Salmon: Season the salmon fillet with salt and pepper. In a skillet, heat 1 tbsp olive oil over medium heat, then cook the salmon for 4-5 minutes per side until cooked through. Remove and let cool slightly, then flake into chunks.

2. Prepare Dressing: In a small bowl, mix remaining olive oil, lemon juice, salt, and pepper.

3. Assemble Salad: In a large bowl, add arugula, cherry tomatoes, and flaked salmon. Drizzle with dressing and toss gently. Serve: Plate and enjoy.

4. Serve: Plate and enjoy.

Nutritional Breakdown (Estimated per serving)
Calories: 360 kcal, Protein: 24 g, Fat: 18 g, Carbs: 10 g

Sautéed Shrimp & Avocado Salad

 Prep Time: 5 minutes   Cook Time: 5 minutes   Total Time: 10 minutes

 Yield: 2 servings

Ingredients

- 1 cup shrimp, peeled and deveined
- 1 avocado, diced
- 2 cups baby spinach
- 1 tbsp olive oil
- 1 tbsp lime juice
- Salt and pepper, to taste

Instructions

1. Sauté Shrimp: Heat 1 tbsp olive oil in a skillet over medium heat. Season the shrimp with salt and pepper, then cook for 2-3 minutes on each side until pink and opaque. Remove and let cool slightly.

2. Prepare Dressing: In a small bowl, mix lime juice, salt, and pepper.

3. Assemble Salad: In a large bowl, combine spinach, diced avocado, and cooked shrimp. Drizzle with dressing and toss gently.

4. Serve: Plate and enjoy immediately.

Nutritional Breakdown (Estimated per serving)
Calories: 300 kcal, Protein: 20 g, Fat: 18 g, Carbs: 8 g

Warm Steak & Arugula Salad

 Prep Time: 5 minutes   Cook Time: 8 minutes   Total Time: 13 minutes

 Yield: 2 servings

Ingredients

- 1 small steak (such as flank or sirloin)
- 2 cups arugula
- ½ cup cherry tomatoes, halved
- 1 tbsp balsamic vinegar
- 1 tbsp olive oil
- Salt and pepper, to taste

Instructions

1. Season and Cook Steak: Season the steak with salt and pepper. In a skillet, heat olive oil over medium-high heat, then cook the steak for 3-4 minutes on each side to desired doneness. Let rest for a few minutes, then slice thinly.

2. Prepare Dressing: In a small bowl, whisk balsamic vinegar with a pinch of salt and pepper.

3. Assemble Salad: In a large bowl, add arugula, cherry tomatoes, and steak slices. Drizzle with dressing and toss gently.

4. Serve: Plate and enjoy.

Nutritional Breakdown (Estimated per serving)
Calories: 300 kcal, Protein: 18 g, Fat: 18 g, Carbs: 16 g

Sautéed Tuna & Quinoa Salad

 Prep Time: 5 minutes *Cook Time: 15 minutes* *Total Time: 20 minutes* *Yield: 2 servings*

Ingredients

- 1 tuna steak
- ½ cup dry quinoa
- 1 cup water
- 1 cup mixed greens
- 1 tbsp soy sauce
- 1 tbsp olive oil
- Salt and pepper, to taste

Instructions

1. Cook Quinoa: In a small pot, combine ½ cup quinoa with 1 cup water and a pinch of salt. Bring to a boil over medium-high heat, then reduce heat to low, cover, and simmer for 12-15 minutes until the water is absorbed and the quinoa is tender. Remove from heat and let sit, covered, for 5 minutes. Fluff with a fork and set aside to cool slightly.

2. Season and Sear Tuna: Season the tuna steak with salt, pepper, and soy sauce. In a skillet, heat olive oil over medium-high heat and sear tuna for 2-3 minutes on each side until cooked to your preferred doneness. Remove from the skillet and slice thinly.

3. Assemble Salad: In a large bowl, combine the cooked quinoa, mixed greens, and sliced tuna. Toss gently to combine.

4. Serve: Divide between plates and enjoy immediately.

Nutritional Breakdown (Estimated per serving)
Calories: 350 kcal, Protein: 28 g, Fat: 14 g, Carbs: 20 g

Grilled Shrimp & Mango Salad

 Prep Time: 5 minutes *Cook Time: 5 minutes* *Total Time: 10 minutes* *Yield: 2 servings*

Ingredients

- 1 cup shrimp, peeled and deveined
- 1 mango, diced
- 2 cups romaine lettuce, chopped
- 1 tbsp olive oil
- 1 tbsp lime juice
- Salt and pepper, to taste

Instructions

1. Grill Shrimp: Toss shrimp with olive oil, salt, and pepper. Grill over medium heat for 2-3 minutes per side until pink. Remove and let cool.

2. Assemble Salad: In a large bowl, combine romaine, diced mango, and grilled shrimp. Drizzle with lime juice and toss to coat.

3. Serve: Plate and enjoy.

Nutritional Breakdown (Estimated per serving)
Calories: 280 kcal, Protein: 18 g, Fat: 12 g, Carbs: 22 g

CHAPTER 10: SNACKS AND APPETIZERS

Spicy Hummus with Veggie Sticks

 Prep Time: 10 minutes   Total Time: 10 minutes   Yield: 4servings

Ingredients

- 1 cup canned chickpeas, rinsed and drained
- 2 tbsp tahini
- 1 tbsp olive oil
- 1 clove garlic
- 1 tbsp lemon juice
- ½ tsp cayenne pepper
- Salt, to taste
- Veggie sticks (carrots, celery, bell peppers)

Instructions

1. **Blend Hummus:** In a food processor, combine chickpeas, tahini, olive oil, garlic, lemon juice, cayenne pepper, and salt. Blend until smooth, adding a little water if needed for desired consistency.
2. **Serve:** Scoop the hummus into a bowl and serve with veggie sticks.

Nutritional Breakdown (Estimated per serving)
Calories: 150 kcal, Protein: 6 g, Fat: 8 g, Carbs: 14 g

Avocado Toast with Smoked Salmon

Prep Time: 5 minutes Total Time: 5 minutes Yield: 2 servings

Ingredients

- 1 ripe avocado
- 2 slices whole-grain bread, toasted
- 2 oz smoked salmon
- Salt and pepper, to taste
- Optional: fresh dill for garnish

Instructions

1. **Prepare Avocado:** Mash the avocado in a bowl and season with salt and pepper.
2. **Assemble Toast:** Spread the mashed avocado on each slice of toast. Top with smoked salmon and garnish with dill if desired.
3. **Serve:** Plate and enjoy immediately.

Nutritional Breakdown (Estimated per serving)
Calories: 200 kcal, Protein: 10 g, Fat: 12 g, Carbs: 12 g

Stuffed Mini Bell Peppers with Goat Cheese

Ingredients

- 10 mini bell peppers, halved and seeds removed
- ½ cup goat cheese
- 1 tbsp fresh chives, chopped

 Prep Time: 10 minutes Total Time: 10 minutes  Yield: 4servings

Instructions

1. **Fill Peppers:** Spread a small amount of goat cheese into each mini bell pepper half.
2. **Garnish:** Sprinkle chopped chives over the cheese.
3. **Serve:** Arrange on a plate and serve immediately.

Nutritional Breakdown (Estimated per serving)
Calories: 100 kcal, Protein: 4 g, Fat: 7 g, Carbs: 6 g

Energy-Boosting Trail Mix

Ingredients

- ¼ cup almonds
- ¼ cup walnuts
- ¼ cup pumpkin seeds
- ¼ cup dried cranberries
- ¼ cup dark chocolate chips

 Prep Time: 5 minutes Total Time: 5 minutes Yield: 4 servings

Instructions

1. **Mix Ingredients:** In a bowl, combine almonds, walnuts, pumpkin seeds, dried cranberries, and dark chocolate chips.
2. **Serve:** Divide into individual servings or store in an airtight container for later.

Nutritional Breakdown (Estimated per serving)
Calories: 180 kcal, Protein: 6 g, Fat: 12 g, Carbs: 14 g

Greek Yogurt Dip with Cucumber Slices

Ingredients

- 1 cup Greek yogurt
- 1 clove garlic, minced
- 1 tbsp fresh dill, chopped
- 1 tbsp lemon juice
- Salt and pepper, to taste
- 1 cucumber, sliced

 Prep Time: 5 minutes Total Time: 5 minutes Yield: 4servings

Instructions

1. **Prepare Dip:** In a bowl, mix Greek yogurt, garlic, dill, lemon juice, salt, and pepper. Stir until well combined.
2. **Serve:** Place the dip in a bowl and serve with cucumber slices.

Nutritional Breakdown (Estimated per serving)
Calories: 120 kcal, Protein: 8 g, Fat: 4 g, Carbs: 12 g

Almond Butter & Banana Bites

 Prep Time: 5 minutes    *Total Time: 5 minutes*   *Yield: 4servings*

Ingredients

- 1 banana, sliced
- 2 tbsp almond butter

Instructions

1. **Prepare Bites:** Spread a small amount of almond butter on one banana slice, then top with another slice to form a bite-sized sandwich. Repeat for all slices.
2. **Serve:** Arrange on a plate and serve immediately

> **Nutritional Breakdown (Estimated per serving)**
> Calories: 180 kcal, Protein: 4 g, Fat: 8 g, Carbs: 24 g

Spicy Roasted Chickpeas

 Prep Time: 5 minutes   *Cook Time: 20 minutes*   *Total Time: 25 minutes*
 Yield: 4 servings

Ingredients

- 1 can chickpeas, rinsed and drained
- 1 tbsp olive oil
- ½ tsp paprika
- ½ tsp garlic powder
- Salt and pepper, to taste

Instructions

1. **Preheat Oven:** Preheat oven to 400°F (200°C).
2. **Season Chickpeas:** In a bowl, toss chickpeas with olive oil, paprika, garlic powder, salt, and pepper.
3. **Roast:** Spread chickpeas on a baking sheet and roast for 20 minutes, shaking halfway through, until crispy.
4. **Serve:** Let cool slightly and serve warm or at room temperature.

> **Nutritional Breakdown (Estimated per serving)**
> Calories: 100 kcal, Protein: 5 g, Fat: 2 g, Carbs: 18 g

Caprese Skewers

 Prep Time: 5 minutes   *Total Time: 5 minutes*   *Yield: 4 servings*

Ingredients

- 10 cherry tomatoes
- 10 small fresh mozzarella balls
- 10 fresh basil leaves
- 1 tbsp balsamic glaze

Instructions

1. **Assemble Skewers:** Thread a cherry tomato, mozzarella ball, and basil leaf onto a toothpick. Repeat for remaining ingredients.
2. **Drizzle with Balsamic:** Arrange on a plate and drizzle with balsamic glaze.
3. **Serve:** Serve immediately.

> **Nutritional Breakdown (Estimated per serving)**
> Calories: 150 kcal, Protein: 6 g, Fat: 10 g, Carbs: 8 g

CHAPTER 11: VEGAN AND VEGETARIAN OPTIONS

Sweet Potato & Black Bean Tacos

 Prep Time: 5 minutes Cook Time: 15 minutes Total Time: 20 minutes
 Yield: 4 servings

Ingredients
- 1 large sweet potato, diced
- 1 can black beans, drained and rinsed
- 1 tbsp olive oil
- 1 tsp cumin
- Salt and pepper, to taste
- 8 small corn tortillas

Instructions

1. **Heat Oil:** In a large skillet over medium heat, add olive oil and heat until shimmering, about 1 minute.
2. **Cook Sweet Potato:** Add diced sweet potato to the skillet and season with salt and pepper. Cook for 10-12 minutes, stirring occasionally, until tender and golden brown.
3. **Add Black Beans and Seasoning:** Add black beans to the skillet along with cumin. Stir well and cook for another 2-3 minutes until the beans are heated through.
4. **Assemble Tacos:** Warm tortillas in a separate skillet or microwave. Divide the sweet potato and black bean mixture among the tortillas.
5. **Serve:** Serve warm, optionally garnished with fresh cilantro or a squeeze of lime.

Nutritional Breakdown (Estimated per serving)
Calories: 250 kcal, Protein: 8 g, Fat: 8 g, Carbs: 38 g

Chickpea & Spinach Stuffed Bell Peppers

 Prep Time: 5 minutes Cook Time: 20 minutes Total Time: 25 minutes
Yield: 4 servings

Ingredients
- 4 bell peppers, tops removed and seeds cleaned
- 1 can chickpeas, drained and rinsed
- 2 cups fresh spinach, chopped
- 1 tbsp olive oil
- Salt and pepper, to taste

Instructions

1. **Preheat Oven:** Preheat oven to 375°F (190°C).
2. **Prepare Chickpea and Spinach Filling:** In a skillet over medium heat, add olive oil and heat until shimmering. Add chickpeas and cook for 2-3 minutes. Add spinach, stir to combine, and cook until spinach is wilted, about 2 minutes. Season with salt and pepper.
3. **Stuff Peppers:** Arrange bell peppers upright in a baking dish. Spoon the chickpea and spinach mixture into each pepper, filling them generously.
4. **Bake:** Place the baking dish in the oven and bake for 15-20 minutes until the peppers are tender.
5. **Serve:** Allow to cool slightly before serving. Enjoy warm.

Nutritional Breakdown (Estimated per serving)
Calories: 220 kcal, Protein: 10 g, Fat: 6 g, Carbs: 34 g

Avocado & Black Bean Salad

 Prep Time: 10 minutes   Total Time: 10 minutes Yield: 2 servings

Ingredients

- 1 avocado, diced
- 1 can black beans, drained and rinsed
- 1 cup cherry tomatoes, halved
- ¼ cup red onion, diced
- 1 tbsp lime juice
- Salt and pepper, to taste

Instructions

1. **Prepare Ingredients:** Dice the avocado, halve the cherry tomatoes, and dice the red onion.
2. **Combine Ingredients:** In a large mixing bowl, combine the diced avocado, black beans, cherry tomatoes, and red onion.
3. **Add Lime Juice and Seasoning:** Drizzle with lime juice and season with salt and pepper.
4. **Toss Salad:** Gently toss the salad to combine all ingredients, being careful not to mash the avocado.
5. **Serve:** Divide into servings and enjoy fresh. This salad can also be served with tortilla chips.

Nutritional Breakdown (Estimated per serving)
Calories: 200 kcal, Protein: 6 g, Fat: 12 g, Carbs: 18 g

Stuffed Portobello Mushrooms

 Prep Time: 5 minutes   Cook Time: 15 minutes   Total Time: 20 minutes
 Yield: 4 servings

Ingredients

- 4 large portobello mushrooms, stems removed
- 1 cup cherry tomatoes, diced
- ½ cup breadcrumbs (or vegan alternative)
- 1 tbsp olive oil
- 1 tbsp fresh basil, chopped
- Salt and pepper, to taste

Instructions

1. **Preheat Oven:** Preheat oven to 400°F (200°C).
2. **Prepare Filling:** In a bowl, combine diced tomatoes, breadcrumbs, olive oil, basil, salt, and pepper. Stir until evenly mixed.
3. **Stuff Mushrooms:** Arrange portobello mushrooms on a baking sheet. Spoon the filling mixture evenly into each mushroom cap.
4. **Bake:** Place the baking sheet in the oven and bake for 15 minutes, or until the mushrooms are tender and the filling is golden.
5. **Serve:** Let cool slightly before serving. Garnish with extra basil if desired.

Nutritional Breakdown (Estimated per serving)
Calories: 180 kcal, Protein: 6 g, Fat: 10 g, Carbs: 18 g

Lentil & Veggie Stir-Fry

 Prep Time: 10 minutes *Cook Time: 15 minutes* *Total Time: 20 minutes*
 Yield: 4 servings

Ingredients

- 1 cup dry lentils
- 1 cup bell peppers, sliced
- 1 cup zucchini, diced
- 1 tbsp olive oil
- 1 tsp soy sauce
- Salt and pepper, to taste

Instructions

1. Cook Lentils: In a pot, combine 1 cup lentils with 2 cups water and a pinch of salt. Bring to a boil, then reduce heat and simmer for 15 minutes until tender. Drain and set aside.

2. Sauté Vegetables: In a skillet over medium heat, add olive oil and heat until shimmering. Add bell peppers and zucchini and cook for 5-7 minutes, stirring occasionally, until tender.

3. Add Lentils and Seasoning: Add the cooked lentils to the skillet along with soy sauce, salt, and pepper. Stir well and cook for 2-3 minutes to combine flavors.

4. Serve: Divide into bowls and serve warm.

Nutritional Breakdown (Estimated per serving)
Calories: 240 kcal, Protein: 12 g, Fat: 6 g, Carbs: 38 g

Creamy Coconut Curry Cauliflower

 Prep Time: 5 minutes *Cook Time: 15 minutes* *Total Time: 20 minutes*
Yield: 4 servings

Ingredients

- 1 small head of cauliflower, cut into florets
- 1 cup coconut milk
- 1 tbsp curry powder
- Salt and pepper, to taste

Instructions

1. Combine Ingredients: In a large pot, add cauliflower florets, coconut milk, curry powder, salt, and pepper.

2. Simmer: Bring the mixture to a gentle simmer over medium heat. Cover and cook for 12-15 minutes until cauliflower is tender. Stir occasionally.

3. Serve: Divide into bowls and enjoy warm.

Nutritional Breakdown (Estimated per serving)
Calories: 200 kcal, Protein: 4 g, Fat: 12 g, Carbs: 18 g

Roasted Chickpeas with Paprika

 Prep Time: 5 minutes *Cook Time: 20 minutes* *Total Time: 25 minutes*

 Yield: 4 servings

Ingredients

- 1 can chickpeas, drained and rinsed
- 1 tbsp olive oil
- ½ tsp smoked paprika
- Salt and pepper, to taste

Instructions

1. **Preheat Oven:** Preheat oven to 400°F (200°C).
2. **Season Chickpeas:** In a bowl, toss chickpeas with olive oil, smoked paprika, salt, and pepper.
3. **Roast:** Spread chickpeas in an even layer on a baking sheet. Roast for 20 minutes, shaking halfway through, until crispy.
4. **Serve:** Let cool slightly before serving. Enjoy warm or at room temperature.

Nutritional Breakdown (Estimated per serving)
Calories: 120 kcal, Protein: 6 g, Fat: 4 g, Carbs: 18 g

Zucchini Noodles with Basil Pesto

 Prep Time: 5 minutes *Cook Time: 5 minutes* *Total Time: 10 minutes*

Yield: 2` servings

Ingredients

- 2 zucchinis, spiralized into noodles
- ¼ cup fresh basil
- 2 tbsp olive oil
- 1 clove garlic
- Salt and pepper

Instructions

1. **Prepare Pesto:** In a food processor, combine fresh basil, olive oil, garlic, salt, and pepper. Blend until smooth and creamy. Adjust seasoning as needed.
2. **Toss Zucchini Noodles:** In a large bowl, add the zucchini noodles and pour the basil pesto over them. Toss gently until the noodles are fully coated with the pesto sauce.
3. **Serve:** Divide the pesto-coated zucchini noodles between plates and enjoy fresh. Garnish with extra basil or a sprinkle of crushed nuts for added texture, if desired.

Nutritional Breakdown (Estimated per serving)
Calories: 180 kcal, Protein: 4 g, Fat: 14 g, Carbs: 10 g

CHAPTER 12: ENERGY RESTORATION RECIPES

Berry Chia Smoothie Bowl

 Prep Time: 5 minutes   Total Time: 5 minutes   Yield: 2 servings

Ingredients

- 1 cup mixed berries (strawberries, blueberries, raspberries)
- 1 cup almond milk
- 1 tbsp chia seeds
- 1 tbsp almond butter
- 1 banana, sliced
- Optional toppings: sliced almonds, extra berries

Instructions

1. **Blend Ingredients:** In a blender, combine mixed berries, almond milk, chia seeds, almond butter, and banana. Blend until smooth and creamy.
2. **Serve and Top:** Pour the smoothie into bowls and add desired toppings such as sliced almonds and fresh berries for added texture. Enjoy immediately.

Nutritional Breakdown (Estimated per serving)
Calories: 250 kcal, Protein: 8 g, Fat: 6 g, Carbs: 42 g

Overnight Oats with Walnuts and Blueberries

 Prep Time: 5 minutes   Chill Time: 4 hours or overnight   Total Time: 4 hours   Yield: 2 servings

Ingredients

- 1 cup rolled oats
- 1 cup almond milk
- 1 tbsp chia seeds
- 1 tbsp maple syrup
- ½ cup blueberries
- ¼ cup walnuts, chopped

Instructions

1. **Combine Ingredients:** In a bowl or jar, mix rolled oats, almond milk, chia seeds, and maple syrup. Stir well to combine.
2. **Chill:** Cover and refrigerate for at least 4 hours, or overnight, until the oats soften and absorb the liquid.
3. **Serve:** Divide into bowls and top with fresh blueberries and chopped walnuts before serving.

Nutritional Breakdown (Estimated per serving)
Calories: 280 kcal, Protein: 8 g, Fat: 12 g, Carbs: 36 g

Energy-Boosting Green Smoothie

 Prep Time: 5 minutes   *Total Time: 5 minutes*   *Yield: 2 servings*

Ingredients

- 1 cup spinach
- 1 green apple, chopped
- 1 cup coconut water
- 1 tbsp almond butter
- ½ avocado

Instructions

1. **Blend Ingredients:** Place spinach, apple, coconut water, almond butter, and avocado in a blender. Blend until smooth and creamy.
2. **Serve:** Pour into glasses and enjoy immediately.

> *Nutritional Breakdown (Estimated per serving)*
> Calories: 200 kcal, Protein: 6 g, Fat: 8 g, Carbs: 28 g

Avocado & Hummus Toast

 Prep Time: 5 minutes   *Total Time: 5 minutes*   *Yield: 2 servings*

Ingredients

- 2 slices whole-grain bread, toasted
- ½ avocado, sliced
- 2 tbsp hummus
- Salt and pepper, to taste
- Optional: sprinkle of red pepper flakes

Instructions

1. **Assemble Toast:** Spread 1 tbsp of hummus on each slice of toast, then layer with avocado slices.
2. **Season:** Sprinkle with salt, pepper, and optional red pepper flakes for added flavor.
3. **Serve:** Plate and enjoy immediately.

> *Nutritional Breakdown (Estimated per serving)*
> Calories: 250 kcal, Protein: 8 g, Fat: 14 g, Carbs: 24 g

Greek Yogurt Parfait with Honey and Nuts

 Prep Time: 5 minutes   *Total Time: 5 minutes*   *Yield: 2 servings*

Ingredients

- 1 cup Greek yogurt
- 1 tbsp honey
- ¼ cup mixed nuts (almonds, walnuts, pistachios), chopped
- ¼ cup fresh berries

Instructions

1. **Layer Ingredients:** In a bowl or parfait glass, add a layer of Greek yogurt, followed by a drizzle of honey, a sprinkle of mixed nuts, and fresh berries.
2. **Repeat Layers:** Continue layering until all ingredients are used.
3. **Serve:** Enjoy immediately as a refreshing energy-restoring snack.

> *Nutritional Breakdown (Estimated per serving)*
> Calories: 230 kcal, Protein: 12 g, Fat: 8 g, Carbs: 28 g

Quinoa and Edamame Power Bowl

 Prep Time: 5 minutes Cook Time: 15 minutes Total Time: 20 minutes

 Yield: 2 servings

Ingredients

- ½ cup dry quinoa
- 1 cup water
- ½ cup shelled edamame
- ½ cup cucumber, diced
- 1 tbsp lemon juice
- 1 tbsp olive oil
- Salt and pepper, to taste

Instructions

1. **Cook Quinoa:** In a small pot, combine quinoa with water and a pinch of salt. Bring to a boil, then reduce heat and simmer for 12-15 minutes until water is absorbed. Fluff with a fork.
2. **Assemble Bowl:** In a large bowl, combine cooked quinoa, edamame, and diced cucumber.
3. **Add Dressing:** Drizzle with lemon juice and olive oil, then season with salt and pepper. Toss to combine.
4. **Serve:** Divide into servings and enjoy warm or cold.

Nutritional Breakdown (Estimated per serving)
Calories: 320 kcal, Protein: 12 g, Fat: 10 g, Carbs: 42 g

Banana Almond Energy Bites

 Prep Time: 5 minutes Cook Time: 15 minutes Total Time: 20 minutes

Yield: 2 servings

Ingredients

- 1 cup rolled oats
- 1 ripe banana, mashed
- 2 tbsp almond butter
- 1 tbsp maple syrup
- 1 tbsp chia seeds

Instructions

1. **Mix Ingredients:** In a mixing bowl, combine rolled oats, mashed banana, almond butter, maple syrup, and chia seeds. Stir until well blended.
2. **Form Bites:** Scoop out small portions and roll into bite-sized balls.
3. **Chill:** Place in the refrigerator for at least 15 minutes to firm up.
4. **Serve:** Enjoy as a quick energy-boosting snack.

Nutritional Breakdown (Estimated per serving)
Calories: 100 kcal, Protein: 3 g, Fat: 5 g, Carbs: 12 g

Vegetable & Hummus Wrap

 Prep Time: 5 minutes Total Time: 5 minutes Yield: 2 servings

Ingredients

- 2 large whole-grain wraps
- 4 tbsp hummus
- ½ cup shredded carrots
- ½ cup cucumber slices
- ¼ cup red bell pepper, thinly sliced
- Salt and pepper, to taste

Instructions

1. **Spread Hummus:** Spread 2 tbsp of hummus onto each wrap.
2. **Add Vegetables:** Layer shredded carrots, cucumber slices, and red bell pepper on top of the hummus.
3. **Season and Roll:** Season with salt and pepper, then roll up the wrap tightly.
4. **Serve:** Cut in half and enjoy immediately as a refreshing snack or light meal.

Nutritional Breakdown (Estimated per serving)
Calories: 220 kcal, Protein: 6 g, Fat: 10 g, Carbs: 24 g

CHAPTER 13: ENERGY DETOX RECIPES

Green Detox Smoothie

 Prep Time: 5 minutes   Total Time: 5 minutes   Yield: 2 servings

Ingredients

- 1 cup spinach
- 1 green apple, chopped
- ½ cucumber, chopped
- 1 tbsp lemon juice
- 1 cup coconut water

Instructions

1. **Blend Ingredients:** In a blender, combine spinach, apple, cucumber, lemon juice, and coconut water. Blend until smooth.
2. **Serve:** Pour into glasses and enjoy immediately for a refreshing, detoxifying boost.

Nutritional Breakdown (Estimated per serving)
Calories: 180 kcal, Protein: 4 g, Fat: 6 g, Carbs: 28 g

Cucumber Mint Detox Water

 Prep Time: 5 minutes   Chill Time: 1 hours   Total Time: 1 hour 5 minutes
 Yield: 4 servings

Ingredients

- 1 cucumber, sliced
- 1 lemon, sliced
- 1 handful fresh mint leaves
- 4 cups water

Instructions

1. **Combine Ingredients:** In a large pitcher, add cucumber slices, lemon slices, and mint leaves. Fill with water.
2. **Chill:** Place in the refrigerator for at least 1 hour to allow flavors to infuse.
3. **Serve:** Pour into glasses and enjoy throughout the day.

Nutritional Breakdown (Estimated per serving)
Calories: 10 kcal, Protein: 0 g, Fat: 0 g, Carbs: 2 g

Beet & Berry Detox Juice

 Prep Time: 5 minutes   Total Time: 5 minutes   Yield: 2 servings

Ingredients

- 1 small beet, peeled and chopped
- ½ cup strawberries
- ½ cup blueberries
- 1 cup water

1. **Blend Ingredients:** In a blender, add beet, strawberries, blueberries, and water. Blend until smooth.
2. **Strain (Optional):** For a smoother juice, strain through a fine mesh sieve.
3. **Serve:** Pour into glasses and enjoy immediately.

Nutritional Breakdown (Estimated per serving)
Calories: 120 kcal, Protein: 3 g, Fat: 1 g, Carbs: 28 g

Turmeric Ginger Detox Tea

 Prep Time: 5 minutes Cook Time: 5minutes Total Time: 10 minutes

 Yield: 2 servings

Ingredients

- 1 tsp turmeric powder
- 1 tsp fresh ginger, grated
- 2 cups water
- 1 tbsp lemon juice
- 1 tsp honey (optional)

Instructions

1. **Simmer Tea:** In a small pot, bring water to a gentle simmer. Add turmeric and ginger, stirring well.

2. **Steep and Strain:** Let simmer for 5 minutes, then strain into mugs.

3. **Add Lemon and Serve:** Stir in lemon juice and honey if desired. Enjoy warm.

> *Nutritional Breakdown (Estimated per serving)*
> Calories: 20 kcal, Protein: 0 g, Fat: 0 g, Carbs: 5 g

Apple Cider Vinegar Detox Drink

 Prep Time: 5 minutes Total Time: 5 minutes Yield: 1 serving

Ingredients

- 1 tbsp apple cider vinegar
- 1 tbsp lemon juice
- 1 tsp honey (optional)
- 1 cup water

Instructions

1. **Combine Ingredients:** In a glass, mix apple cider vinegar, lemon juice, honey (if using), and water. Stir well.
2. **Serve:** Drink immediately for a refreshing detox boost.

> *Nutritional Breakdown (Estimated per serving)*
> Calories: 30 kcal, Protein: 0 g, Fat: 0 g, Carbs: 8 g

Pineapple & Ginger Detox Smoothie

 Prep Time: 5 minutes Total Time: 5 minutes Yield: 2 servings

Ingredients

- 1 cup fresh pineapple, chopped
- 1 small cucumber, chopped
- 1 tsp fresh ginger, grated
- 1 cup coconut water

Instructions

1. **Blend Ingredients:** In a blender, combine pineapple, cucumber, ginger, and coconut water. Blend until smooth.
2. **Serve:** Pour into glasses and enjoy immediately.

> *Nutritional Breakdown (Estimated per serving)*
> Calories: 140 kcal, Protein: 1 g, Fat: 0 g, Carbs: 35 g

CHAPTER 14: SAUCES, DIPS, AND DRESSINGS

Lemon Tahini Dressing

 Prep Time: 5 minutes   Total Time: 5 minutes   Yield: 4 servings

Ingredients

- ¼ cup tahini
- 2 tbsp lemon juice
- 2 tbsp water
- 1 clove garlic, minced
- Salt and pepper, to taste

Instructions

1. **Mix Ingredients:** In a bowl, whisk together tahini, lemon juice, water, and minced garlic until smooth.
2. **Season:** Add salt and pepper to taste, adjusting consistency with a little more water if necessary.
3. **Serve:** Use as a dressing for salads or as a dip for veggies.

Nutritional Breakdown (Estimated per serving)
Calories: 70 kcal, Protein: 2 g, Fat: 6 g, Carbs: 4 g

Garlic Herb Yogurt Sauce

 Prep Time: 5 minutes   Total Time: 5 minutes   Yield: 4 servings

Ingredients

- ½ cup Greek yogurt
- 1 clove garlic, minced
- 1 tbsp fresh dill, chopped
- 1 tbsp fresh parsley, chopped
- Salt and pepper, to taste

Instructions

1. **Combine Ingredients:** In a bowl, mix Greek yogurt, garlic, dill, parsley, salt, and pepper.
2. **Mix Well:** Stir until all ingredients are well combined.
3. **Serve:** Use as a sauce for grilled vegetables, roasted meats, or as a spread for sandwiches.

Nutritional Breakdown (Estimated per serving)
Calories: 50 kcal, Protein: 4 g, Fat: 2 g, Carbs: 5 g

Classic Vinaigrette

 Prep Time: 5 minutes   *Total Time: 5 minutes*   *Yield: 4 serving*

Ingredients

- 3 tbsp olive oil
- 1 tbsp red wine vinegar
- 1 tsp Dijon mustard
- Salt and pepper, to taste

Instructions

1. **Whisk Ingredients:** In a small bowl, whisk together olive oil, red wine vinegar, Dijon mustard, salt, and pepper.
2. **Adjust Seasoning:** Taste and adjust seasoning as desired.
3. **Serve:** Use as a dressing for salads or as a marinade for vegetables.

Nutritional Breakdown (Estimated per serving)
Calories: 60 kcal, Protein: 0 g, Fat: 6 g, Carbs: 1 g

Mango Salsa

 Prep Time: 5 minutes   *Total Time: 5 minutes*   *Yield: 4 servings*

Ingredients

- 1 mango, diced
- ¼ cup red bell pepper, diced
- 1 tbsp red onion, finely chopped
- 1 tbsp cilantro, chopped
- 1 tsp lime juice

Instructions

1. **Combine Ingredients:** In a bowl, mix diced mango, red bell pepper, red onion, cilantro, and lime juice.
2. **Toss and Mix:** Stir to combine all ingredients evenly.
3. **Serve:** Serve as a topping for fish, chicken, or as a refreshing dip for chips.

Nutritional Breakdown (Estimated per serving)
Calories: 40 kcal, Protein: 0 g, Fat: 0 g, Carbs: 10 g

Spicy Cashew Sauce

 Prep Time: 5 minutes   *Total Time: 5 minutes*   *Yield: 4 serving*

Ingredients

- ¼ cup raw cashews, soaked and drained
- 2 tbsp water
- 1 tsp hot sauce
- 1 tbsp lime juice

Instructions

1. **Blend Ingredients:** In a blender, combine soaked cashews, water, hot sauce, and lime juice. Blend until smooth.
2. **Adjust Consistency:** Add a little more water if needed for desired consistency.
3. **Serve:** Use as a sauce for veggie bowls, wraps, or as a creamy dip.

Nutritional Breakdown (Estimated per serving)
Calories: 80 kcal, Protein: 2 g, Fat: 6 g, Carbs: 4 g

CHAPTER 15: GUILT-FREE DESSERTS

Chocolate Avocado Mousse

 Prep Time: 5 minutes   Chill Time: 30 minutes   Total Time: 35 minutes

Yield: 4 servings

Instructions

Ingredients

- 2 ripe avocados
- ¼ cup cocoa powder
- 3 tbsp maple syrup
- 1 tsp vanilla extract

1. **Prepare Ingredients:** Scoop out avocado flesh and place it in a blender or food processor.
2. **Blend:** Add cocoa powder, maple syrup, and vanilla extract. Blend until smooth and creamy, stopping to scrape down the sides if needed.
3. **Adjust Sweetness:** Taste and add more maple syrup if desired.
4. **Chill and Serve:** Spoon into bowls and refrigerate for at least 30 minutes before serving. Enjoy with fresh berries or a sprinkle of cacao nibs.

Nutritional Breakdown (Estimated per serving)
Calories: 180 kcal, Protein: 3 g, Fat: 12 g, Carbs: 16 g

Banana Nice Cream

 Prep Time: 5 minutes Freez Time: 2 hours   Total Time: 2 hours 5 minutes

Yield: 4 servings

Instructions

Ingredients

- 2 ripe bananas, sliced and frozen
- 1 tsp vanilla extract

1. **Freeze Bananas:** Place sliced bananas in a freezer-safe bag and freeze for at least 2 hours.
2. **Blend:** Add frozen banana slices and vanilla extract to a blender. Blend until creamy and smooth, stopping to scrape down the sides as needed.
3. **Serve Immediately:** Scoop into bowls and enjoy. Add toppings like berries or a sprinkle of cinnamon for extra flavor.

Nutritional Breakdown (Estimated per serving)
Calories: 100 kcal, Protein: 1 g, Fat: 0 g, Carbs: 26 g

Coconut Chia Pudding

 Prep Time: 5 minutes   *Chill Time: 4hours*   *Total Time: 4 hours 5 minutes*

Yield: 4 serving

Ingredients

- 1 cup coconut milk
- 3 tbsp chia seeds
- 1 tbsp maple syrup
- ½ tsp vanilla extract

Instructions

1. **Combine Ingredients:** In a bowl, whisk together coconut milk, chia seeds, maple syrup, and vanilla extract.
2. **Let Thicken:** Cover and refrigerate for at least 4 hours or overnight, stirring once after the first 30 minutes to prevent clumping.
3. **Serve:** Spoon into bowls and top with fresh fruit or shredded coconut.

> **Nutritional Breakdown (Estimated per serving)**
> Calories: 150 kcal, Protein: 3 g, Fat: 8 g, Carbs: 16 g

Greek Yogurt with Honey and Berries

 Prep Time: 5 minutes   *Total Time: 5 minutes*   *Yield: 2 servings*

Ingredients

- 1 cup Greek yogurt
- 1 tbsp honey
- ½ cup mixed berries

Instructions

1. **Layer Ingredients:** In a bowl, add Greek yogurt, drizzle with honey, and top with mixed berries.
2. **Serve:** Stir lightly if desired and enjoy immediately.

> **Nutritional Breakdown (Estimated per serving)**
> Calories: 120 kcal, Protein: 8 g, Fat: 2 g, Carbs: 18 g

Baked Cinnamon Pears

 Prep Time: 5 minutes   *Cook Time: 15 minutes*   *Total Time: 5 minutes*

 Yield: 2 servings

Ingredients

- 2 pears, halved and cored
- 1 tsp cinnamon
- 1 tbsp honey

Instructions

1. **Preheat Oven:** Preheat oven to 350°F (175°C).
2. **Prepare Pears:** Place pear halves in a baking dish. Sprinkle with cinnamon and drizzle with honey.
3. **Bake:** Bake for 15 minutes until pears are tender.
4. **Serve:** Serve warm with a spoonful of yogurt or a sprinkle of granola.

> **Nutritional Breakdown (Estimated per serving)**
> Calories: 100 kcal, Protein: 0 g, Fat: 0 g, Carbs: 26 g

Apple Nachos

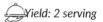 *Prep Time: 5 minutes*   *Total Time: 5 minutes*   *Yield: 2 serving*

Ingredients

- 1 apple, sliced
- 1 tbsp almond butter
- 1 tbsp shredded coconut
- 1 tsp dark chocolate chips

Instructions

1. Arrange Apple Slices: Spread apple slices on a plate in a single layer.

2. Drizzle and Sprinkle: Warm almond butter slightly if needed and drizzle over apple slices. Sprinkle with shredded coconut and dark chocolate chips.

3. Serve: Enjoy immediately as a refreshing and nutritious snack.

> **Nutritional Breakdown (Estimated per serving)**
> Calories: 130 kcal, Protein: 2 g, Fat: 4 g, Carbs: 24 g

Date & Nut Energy Balls

Prep Time: 10 minutes   *Chill Time: 15 minutes*   *Total Time: 25 minutes*   *Yield: 12 balls*

Ingredients

- 1 cup pitted dates
- ½ cup almonds
- ½ cup walnuts
- 1 tbsp cocoa powder

Instructions

1. Blend Ingredients: In a food processor, combine dates, almonds, walnuts, and cocoa powder. Pulse until mixture is crumbly and sticks together.

2. Form Balls: Scoop out 1 tablespoon of the mixture and roll into a ball. Repeat with remaining mixture.

3. Chill and Serve: Place energy balls in the refrigerator for at least 15 minutes before serving.

> **Nutritional Breakdown (Estimated per serving)**
> Calories: 80 kcal, Protein: 2 g, Fat: 4 g, Carbs: 10 g

Frozen Yogurt Bark

Prep Time: 5 minutes   *Freeze Time: 2 hours*   *Total Time: 2 hours 5 minutes*   *Yield: 4 servings*

Ingredients

- 1 cup Greek yogurt
- 1 tbsp honey
- ¼ cup mixed berries
- 1 tbsp chopped nuts

Instructions

1. Spread Yogurt: Line a baking sheet with parchment paper. Spread yogurt evenly over the paper.

2. Add Toppings: Drizzle honey over yogurt, then sprinkle with berries and nuts.

3. Freeze: Place in the freezer for at least 2 hours until firm.

4. Break and Serve: Break into pieces and serve immediately. Store leftovers in the freezer.

> **Nutritional Breakdown (Estimated per serving)**
> Calories: 90 kcal, Protein: 4 g, Fat: 2 g, Carbs: 12 g

Pumpkin Spice Chia Pudding

 Prep Time: 10 minutes *Chill Time: 4 hours* *Total Time: 4 hours 5 minutes*
 Yield: 4 servings

Ingredients

- 1 cup almond milk
- 3 tbsp chia seeds
- ¼ cup pumpkin puree
- ½ tsp pumpkin spice
- 1 tbsp maple syrup

Instructions

1. **Combine Ingredients:** In a bowl, whisk almond milk, chia seeds, pumpkin puree, pumpkin spice, and maple syrup.
2. **Refrigerate:** Cover and refrigerate for at least 4 hours, stirring after 30 minutes to prevent clumping.
3. **Serve:** Spoon into bowls and top with a sprinkle of cinnamon.

Nutritional Breakdown (Estimated per serving)
Calories: 130 kcal, Protein: 3 g, Fat: 6 g, Carbs: 16 g

Chocolate Dipped Strawberries

 Prep Time: 5 minutes *Chill Time: 10 minutes* *Total Time: 15 minutes*
 Yield: 2 servings

Ingredients

- ½ cup strawberries
- ¼ cup dark chocolate chips

Instructions

1. **Melt Chocolate:** In a microwave-safe bowl, melt chocolate chips in 20-second intervals, stirring until smooth.
2. **Dip Strawberries:** Dip each strawberry halfway into the melted chocolate, allowing excess to drip off.
3. **Chill:** Place strawberries on a parchment-lined plate and refrigerate for 10 minutes to set the chocolate.
4. **Serve:** Enjoy fresh or store in the refrigerator for up to a day.

Nutritional Breakdown (Estimated per serving)
Calories: 80 kcal, Protein: 1 g, Fat: 4 g, Carbs: 10 g

CHAPTER 16: ENERGY-BOOSTING DRINKS

Matcha Green Tea Latte

 Prep Time: 5 minutes   Total Time: 5 minutes   Yield: 1 serving

Ingredients

- 1 tsp matcha powder
- 1 cup almond milk
- 1 tsp honey or maple syrup (optional)

Instructions

1. **Heat Milk:** In a small pot, warm almond milk over low heat until steaming (do not boil).
2. **Whisk Matcha:** In a cup, whisk matcha powder with a splash of hot water until smooth.
3. **Combine and Sweeten:** Pour warmed milk over matcha, stirring to combine. Add honey or maple syrup if desired.
4. **Serve:** Enjoy warm for a calming energy boost.

Nutritional Breakdown (Estimated per serving)
Calories: 80 kcal, Protein: 2 g, Fat: 3 g, Carbs: 10 g

Berry Spinach Smoothie

 Prep Time: 5 minutes   Total Time: 5 minutes   Yield: 1 serving

Ingredients

- ½ cup mixed berries (strawberries, blueberries)
- 1 cup spinach
- 1 cup almond milk
- ½ banana

Instructions

1. **Blend Ingredients:** In a blender, combine berries, spinach, almond milk, and banana. Blend until smooth.
2. **Serve:** Pour into a glass and enjoy immediately.

Nutritional Breakdown (Estimated per serving)
Calories: 120 kcal, Protein: 3 g, Fat: 1 g, Carbs: 26 g

Minty Green Tea Cooler

 Prep Time: 5 minutes   *Total Time: 5 minutes*  *Yield: 1 serving*

Ingredients

- 1 green tea bag
- 1 cup hot water
- 5-6 fresh mint leaves
- Ice cubes

Instructions

1. **Brew Tea:** Steep green tea bag in hot water for 3-5 minutes.
2. **Add Mint and Ice:** Remove the tea bag, add mint leaves, and let cool. Pour over ice.
3. **Serve:** Enjoy chilled for a refreshing boost.

> **Nutritional Breakdown (Estimated per serving)**
> Calories: 0 kcal, Protein: 0 g, Fat: 0 g, Carbs: 0 g

Ginger Lemon Detox Tea

 Prep Time: 5 minutes   *Total Time: 5 minutes*   *Yield: 1 serving*

Ingredients

- 1 tsp fresh ginger, grated
- 1 tbsp lemon juice
- 1 cup hot water
- 1 tsp honey (optional)

Instructions

1. **Combine Ingredients:** In a mug, add grated ginger and lemon juice.
2. **Pour Hot Water:** Add hot water and stir well.
3. **Sweeten and Serve:** Add honey if desired. Enjoy warm for a refreshing boost.

> **Nutritional Breakdown (Estimated per serving)**
> Calories: 10 kcal, Protein: 0 g, Fat: 0 g, Carbs: 2 g

Golden Turmeric Latte

 Prep Time: 5 minutes   *Total Time: 5 minutes*   *Yield: 1 serving*

Ingredients

- 1 cup coconut milk
- ½ tsp turmeric powder
- ¼ tsp cinnamon
- 1 tsp honey or maple syrup

Instructions

1. **Heat Milk:** In a small pot, combine coconut milk, turmeric, and cinnamon. Heat over low until steaming, stirring frequently.
2. **Sweeten and Serve:** Remove from heat and add honey or maple syrup. Stir well.
3. **Serve:** Pour into a mug and enjoy warm.

> **Nutritional Breakdown (Estimated per serving)**
> Calories: 90 kcal, Protein: 2 g, Fat: 5 g, Carbs: 8 g

Iced Matcha Lemonade

 Prep Time: 5 minutes   Total Time: 5 minutes   Yield: 1 serving

Ingredients

- 1 tsp matcha powder
- ½ cup water
- 1 tbsp lemon juice
- 1 tsp honey
- Ice cubes

Instructions

1. **Mix Matcha:** In a shaker or jar, combine matcha powder and water. Shake until well blended.
2. **Add Lemon and Honey:** Add lemon juice, honey, and ice. Shake again.
3. **Serve:** Pour into a glass and enjoy.

Nutritional Breakdown (Estimated per serving)
Calories: 60 kcal, Protein: 1 g, Fat: 0 g, Carbs: 14 g

Protein-Packed Chocolate Smoothie

 Prep Time: 5 minutes    Total Time: 5 minutes   Yield: 1 serving

Ingredients

- 1 tbsp cocoa powder
- 1 cup almond milk
- ½ banana
- 1 tbsp chia seeds

Instructions

1. **Blend Ingredients:** In a blender, combine cocoa powder, almond milk, banana, and chia seeds. Blend until smooth.
2. **Serve:** Pour into a glass and enjoy immediately.

Nutritional Breakdown (Estimated per serving)
Calories: 150 kcal, Protein: 8 g, Fat: 4 g, Carbs: 20 g

Beet & Orange Energy Juice

 Prep Time: 5 minutes   Total Time: 5 minutes   Yield: 1 serving

Ingredients

- 1 small beet, peeled and chopped
- 1 orange, peeled
- ½ cup water

Instructions

1. **Blend Ingredients:** In a blender, combine beet, orange, and water. Blend until smooth.
2. **Strain (Optional):** For a smoother juice, strain through a fine mesh sieve.
3. **Serve:** Pour into a glass and enjoy immediately.

Nutritional Breakdown (Estimated per serving)
Calories: 110 kcal, Protein: 2 g, Fat: 0 g, Carbs: 25 g

WEEK 1

Day 1
Breakfast: Spinach & Feta Egg Skillet
Lunch: Quick Lemon Herb Chicken Bowl
Dinner: Rosemary Garlic Steak & Veggie Skillet
Snack: Spicy Hummus with Veggie Sticks

Day 2
Breakfast: Tomato & Basil Scrambled Eggs
Lunch: Garlic Shrimp & Spinach Stir-Fry
Dinner: Lemon Herb Chicken & Asparagus
Snack: Avocado Toast with Smoked Salmon

Day 3
Breakfast: Avocado & Smoked Salmon Breakfast Bowl
Lunch: Spicy Chicken & Veggie Lettuce Wraps
Dinner: Garlic Butter Shrimp & Zoodles
Snack: Stuffed Mini Bell Peppers with Goat Cheese

Day 4
Breakfast: Sweet Potato & Sausage Hash
Lunch: Turkey & Zucchini Skillet
Dinner: Honey Dijon Salmon & Green Beans
Snack: Energy-Boosting Trail Mix

Day 5
Breakfast: Kale & Parmesan Breakfast Scramble
Lunch: Lemon Garlic Salmon & Asparagus
Dinner: Spicy Ground Turkey & Cauliflower Rice
Snack: Greek Yogurt Dip with Cucumber Slices

Day 6
Breakfast: Mushroom & Goat Cheese Omelet
Lunch: Ground Beef & Broccoli Stir-Fry
Dinner: Coconut Curry Shrimp & Spinach

Day 7
Breakfast: Apple Cinnamon Oat Skillet
Lunch: Herbed Chicken & Veggie Stir-Fry
Dinner: Balsamic Glazed Chicken & Roasted Carrots
Snack: Almond Butter & Banana Bites

WEEK 2

Day 8
Breakfast: Zucchini & Cheese Egg Bake
Lunch: Egg & Turkey Sausage Zoodle Bowl
Dinner: Tomato Basil Pasta with Ground Beef
Snack: Spicy Roasted Chickpeas

Day 9
Breakfast: Bell Pepper Egg-in-a-Hole
Lunch: Sesame Chicken & Snow Pea Stir-Fry
Dinner: Parmesan-Crusted Pork Chops & Brussels Sprouts
Snack: Spicy Hummus with Veggie Sticks

Day 10
Breakfast: Blueberry Almond Pancake
Lunch: Lemon Garlic Shrimp & Asparagus
Dinner: Mediterranean Chickpea & Spinach Stew
Snack: Avocado Toast with Smoked Salmon

Day 11
Breakfast: Greek Yogurt & Egg Breakfast Skillet
Lunch: Beef & Bell Pepper Fajita Bowl
Dinner: Lemon Garlic Chicken Thighs with Roasted Vegetables
Snack: Stuffed Mini Bell Peppers with Goat Cheese

Day 12
Breakfast: Sautéed Kale & Turkey Bacon Scramble
Lunch: Turkey & Veggie Skillet
Dinner: Beef & Mushroom Stir-Fry
Snack: Almond Butter & Banana Bites

Day 13
Breakfast: Cottage Cheese & Avocado Toast
Lunch: Garlic Mushroom & Chicken Stir-Fry
Dinner: Zesty Shrimp & Cauliflower Rice
Snack: Spicy Roasted Chickpeas

Day 14
Breakfast: Banana Almond Butter Pancakes
Lunch: Cajun Salmon & Spinach Sauté
Dinner: Honey Mustard Pork Chops & Brussels Sprouts
Snack: Caprese Skewers

WEEK 3

Day 15
Breakfast: One-Pan Ham & Cheese Breakfast Roll-Up
Lunch: Zesty Lime Chicken & Avocado Salad
Dinner: Spaghetti Squash Marinara with Ground Turkey
Snack: Spicy Hummus with Veggie Sticks

Day 16
Breakfast: Spicy Egg & Turkey Sausage Skillet
Lunch: Teriyaki Turkey & Vegetable Stir-Fry
Dinner: Thai Basil Chicken Stir-Fry
Snack: Avocado Toast with Smoked Salmon

Day 17
Breakfast: Coconut Chia Pudding with Berries
Lunch: Italian Chicken & Tomato Sauté
Dinner: Garlic Lemon Cod with Steamed Vegetables
Snack: Stuffed Mini Bell Peppers with Goat Cheese

Day 18
Breakfast: Savory Egg & Avocado Quesadilla
Lunch: Honey Mustard Salmon & Zucchini
Dinner: Chicken & Veggie Sheet Pan Dinner
Snack: Energy-Boosting Trail Mix

Day 19
Breakfast: Smoked Salmon & Spinach Breakfast Wrap
Lunch: Greek Chicken & Cauliflower Rice Bowl
Dinner: Ginger Soy Beef & Bok Choy Stir-Fry
Snack: Greek Yogurt Dip with Cucumber Slices

Day 20
Breakfast: Cinnamon Ricotta & Honey Toast
Lunch: Spicy Beef & Broccoli Stir-Fry
Dinner: Herbed Turkey Meatballs with Zucchini Noodles
Snack: Caprese Skewers

Day 21
Breakfast: Spinach & Feta Egg Skillet
Lunch: Quick Lemon Herb Chicken Bowl
Dinner: Lemon Thyme Roast Chicken Thighs
Snack: Almond Butter & Banana Bites

WEEK 4

Day 22
Breakfast: Tomato & Basil Scrambled Eggs
Lunch: Garlic Shrimp & Spinach Stir-Fry
Dinner: Honey Mustard Chicken Breast with Green Beans
Snack: Spicy Roasted Chickpeas

Day 23
Breakfast: Avocado & Smoked Salmon Breakfast Bowl
Lunch: Spicy Chicken & Veggie Lettuce Wraps
Dinner: Garlic Rosemary Chicken Drumsticks
Snack: Spicy Hummus with Veggie Sticks

Day 24
Breakfast: Sweet Potato & Sausage Hash
Lunch: Turkey & Zucchini Skillet
Dinner: Herbed Turkey Cutlets with Spinach
Snack: Avocado Toast with Smoked Salmon

Day 25
Breakfast: Kale & Parmesan Breakfast Scramble
Lunch: Lemon Garlic Salmon & Asparagus
Dinner: Maple Glazed Chicken Tenders
Snack: Stuffed Mini Bell Peppers with Goat Cheese

Day 26
Breakfast: Mushroom & Goat Cheese Omelet
Lunch: Ground Beef & Broccoli Stir-Fry
Dinner: Balsamic Glazed Chicken Breast with Mushrooms
Snack: Almond Butter & Banana Bites

Day 27
Breakfast: Apple Cinnamon Oat Skillet
Lunch: Herbed Chicken & Veggie Stir-Fry
Dinner: Orange Ginger Glazed Duck Breast
Snack: Spicy Roasted Chickpeas

Day 28
Breakfast: Zucchini & Cheese Egg Bake
Lunch: Egg & Turkey Sausage Zoodle Bowl
Dinner: Teriyaki Chicken Thighs with Bell Peppers
Snack: Caprese Skewers

WEEK 5

Day 29
Breakfast: Bell Pepper Egg-in-a-Hole
Lunch: Sesame Chicken & Snow Pea Stir-Fry
Dinner: Herb-Crusted Lamb Chops with Garlic
Spinach
Snack: Energy-Boosting Trail Mix

Day 30
Breakfast: Blueberry Almond Pancake
Lunch: Lemon Garlic Shrimp & Asparagus
Dinner: Garlic Butter Ribeye with Asparagus
Snack: Spicy Hummus with Veggie Sticks

Day 31
Breakfast: Greek Yogurt & Egg Breakfast Skillet
Lunch: Beef & Bell Pepper Fajita Bowl
Dinner: Rosemary & Honey Glazed Pork
Tenderloin
Snack: Almond Butter & Banana Bites

Day 32
Breakfast: Sautéed Kale & Turkey Bacon
Scramble
Lunch: Turkey & Veggie Skillet
Dinner: Seared Lamb Cutlets with Mint Yogurt
Sauce
Snack: Caprese Skewers

Day 33
Breakfast: Cottage Cheese & Avocado Toast
Lunch: Garlic Mushroom & Chicken Stir-Fry
Dinner: Mustard Crusted Pork Chops with
Brussels Sprouts
Snack: Spicy Roasted Chickpeas

Day 34
Breakfast: Banana Almond Butter Pancakes
Lunch: Cajun Salmon & Spinach Sauté
Dinner: Ground Beef & Zucchini Stir-Fry
Snack: Greek Yogurt Dip with Cucumber Slices

Day 35
Breakfast: One-Pan Ham & Cheese Breakfast
Roll-Up
Lunch: Zesty Lime Chicken & Avocado Salad
Dinner: Spiced Lamb Meatballs with Tomato
Sauce
Snack: Avocado Toast with Smoked Salmon

WEEK 6

Day 36
Breakfast: Spicy Egg & Turkey Sausage Skillet
Lunch: Teriyaki Turkey & Vegetable Stir-Fry
Dinner: Honey Glazed Pork Belly with Bok Choy
Snack: Stuffed Mini Bell Peppers with Goat
Cheese

Day 37
Breakfast: Coconut Chia Pudding with Berries
Lunch: Italian Chicken & Tomato Sauté
Dinner: Balsamic Glazed Beef Tenderloin with
Mushrooms
Snack: Almond Butter & Banana Bites

Day 38
Breakfast: Savory Egg & Avocado Quesadilla
Lunch: Honey Mustard Salmon & Zucchini
Dinner: Garlic Herb Lamb Steaks with Mashed
Cauliflower
Snack: Energy-Boosting Trail Mix

Day 39
Breakfast: Smoked Salmon & Spinach
Breakfast Wrap
Lunch: Greek Chicken & Cauliflower Rice Bowl
Dinner: Lemon Herb Salmon with Asparagus
Snack: Spicy Roasted Chickpeas

Day 40
Breakfast: Cinnamon Ricotta & Honey Toast
Lunch: Spicy Beef & Broccoli Stir-Fry
Dinner: Garlic Butter Shrimp & Zoodles
Snack: Caprese Skewers

Day 41
Breakfast: Spinach & Feta Egg Skillet
Lunch: Quick Lemon Herb Chicken Bowl
Dinner: Coconut Curry Cod
Snack: Greek Yogurt Dip with Cucumber Slices

Day 42
Breakfast: Tomato & Basil Scrambled Eggs
Lunch: Garlic Shrimp & Spinach Stir-Fry
Dinner: Chili Lime Grilled Shrimp
Snack: Spicy Hummus with Veggie Sticks

WEEK 7

Day 43
Breakfast: Avocado & Smoked Salmon Breakfast Bowl
Lunch: Spicy Chicken & Veggie Lettuce Wraps
Dinner: Lemon Garlic Tilapia with Spinach
Snack: Caprese Skewers

Day 44
Breakfast: Sweet Potato & Sausage Hash
Lunch: Turkey & Zucchini Skillet
Dinner: Sesame Crusted Seared Tuna
Snack: Almond Butter & Banana Bites

Day 45
Breakfast: Kale & Parmesan Breakfast Scramble
Lunch: Lemon Garlic Salmon & Asparagus
Dinner: Parmesan-Crusted Pork Chops & Brussels Sprouts
Snack: Spicy Hummus with Veggie Sticks

Day 46
Breakfast: Mushroom & Goat Cheese Omelet
Lunch: Ground Beef & Broccoli Stir-Fry
Dinner: Thai Basil Shrimp Stir-Fry
Snack: Energy-Boosting Trail Mix

Day 47
Breakfast: Apple Cinnamon Oat Skillet
Lunch: Herbed Chicken & Veggie Stir-Fry
Dinner: Baked Lemon Pepper Trout
Snack: Greek Yogurt Dip with Cucumber Slices

Day 48
Breakfast: Zucchini & Cheese Egg Bake
Lunch: Egg & Turkey Sausage Zoodle Bowl
Dinner: Honey Dijon Salmon & Green Beans
Snack: Avocado Toast with Smoked Salmon

Day 49
Breakfast: Bell Pepper Egg-in-a-Hole
Lunch: Sesame Chicken & Snow Pea Stir-Fry
Dinner: Beef & Mushroom Stir-Fry
Snack: Spicy Roasted Chickpeas

WEEK 8

Day 50
Breakfast: Blueberry Almond Pancake
Lunch: Lemon Garlic Shrimp & Asparagus
Dinner: Lemon Garlic Chicken Thighs with Roasted Vegetables
Snack: Stuffed Mini Bell Peppers with Goat Cheese

Day 51
Breakfast: Greek Yogurt & Egg Breakfast Skillet
Lunch: Beef & Bell Pepper Fajita Bowl
Dinner: Rosemary Garlic Steak & Veggie Skillet

Day 52
Breakfast: Sautéed Kale & Turkey Bacon Scramble
Lunch: Turkey & Veggie Skillet
Dinner: Teriyaki Chicken Thighs with Bell Peppers
Snack: Caprese Skewers

Day 53
Breakfast: Cottage Cheese & Avocado Toast
Lunch: Garlic Mushroom & Chicken Stir-Fry
Dinner: Coconut Curry Shrimp & Spinach
Snack: Energy-Boosting Trail Mix

Day 54
Breakfast: Banana Almond Butter Pancakes
Lunch: Cajun Salmon & Spinach Sauté
Dinner: Zesty Shrimp & Cauliflower Rice
Snack: Spicy Hummus with Veggie Sticks

Day 55
Breakfast: One-Pan Ham & Cheese Breakfast Roll-Up
Lunch: Zesty Lime Chicken & Avocado Salad
Dinner: Honey Mustard Pork Chops & Brussels Sprouts
Snack: Greek Yogurt Dip with Cucumber Slices

Day 56
Breakfast: Spicy Egg & Turkey Sausage Skillet
Lunch: Teriyaki Turkey & Vegetable Stir-Fry
Dinner: Spaghetti Squash Marinara with Ground Turkey
Snack: Avocado Toast with Smoked Salmon

WEEK 9

Day 57
Breakfast: Coconut Chia Pudding with Berries
Lunch: Italian Chicken & Tomato Sauté
Dinner: Garlic Butter Shrimp & Zoodles
Snack: Stuffed Mini Bell Peppers with Goat Cheese

Day 58
Breakfast: Savory Egg & Avocado Quesadilla
Lunch: Honey Mustard Salmon & Zucchini
Dinner: Spiced Lamb Meatballs with Tomato Sauce
Snack: Spicy Roasted Chickpeas

Day 59
Breakfast: Smoked Salmon & Spinach Breakfast Wrap
Lunch: Greek Chicken & Cauliflower Rice Bowl
Dinner: Seared Lamb Cutlets with Mint Yogurt Sauce
Snack: Almond Butter & Banana Bites

Day 60
Breakfast: Cinnamon Ricotta & Honey Toast
Lunch: Spicy Beef & Broccoli Stir-Fry
Dinner: Lemon Herb Chicken & Asparagus
Snack: Energy-Boosting Trail Mix

Day 61
Breakfast: Spinach & Feta Egg Skillet
Lunch: Ground Beef & Broccoli Stir-Fry
Dinner: Coconut Curry Cod
Snack: Caprese Skewers

Day 62
Breakfast: Tomato & Basil Scrambled Eggs
Lunch: Garlic Shrimp & Spinach Stir-Fry
Dinner: Orange Ginger Glazed Duck Breast
Snack: Greek Yogurt Dip with Cucumber Slices

Day 63
Breakfast: Avocado & Smoked Salmon Breakfast Bowl
Lunch: Cajun Salmon & Spinach Sauté
Dinner: Balsamic Glazed Beef Tenderloin with Mushrooms
Snack: Spicy Hummus with Veggie Sticks

WEEK 10

Day 64
Breakfast: Sweet Potato & Sausage Hash
Lunch: Turkey & Zucchini Skillet
Dinner: Garlic Lemon Cod with Steamed Vegetables
Snack: Almond Butter & Banana Bites

Day 65
Breakfast: Kale & Parmesan Breakfast Scramble
Lunch: Lemon Garlic Salmon & Asparagus
Dinner: Honey Mustard Chicken Breast with Green Beans
Snack: Avocado Toast with Smoked Salmon

Day 66
Breakfast: Mushroom & Goat Cheese Omelet
Lunch: Beef & Bell Pepper Fajita Bowl
Dinner: Thai Basil Shrimp Stir-Fry
Snack: Energy-Boosting Trail Mix

Day 67
Breakfast: Apple Cinnamon Oat Skillet
Lunch: Herbed Chicken & Veggie Stir-Fry
Dinner: Parmesan Crusted Halibut
Snack: Stuffed Mini Bell Peppers with Goat Cheese

Day 68
Breakfast: Zucchini & Cheese Egg Bake
Lunch: Egg & Turkey Sausage Zoodle Bowl
Dinner: Herb-Crusted Lamb Chops with Garlic Spinach
Snack: Caprese Skewers

Day 69
Breakfast: Bell Pepper Egg-in-a-Hole
Lunch: Lemon Garlic Shrimp & Asparagus
Dinner: Turkey & Sweet Potato Stew
Snack: Spicy Roasted Chickpeas

Day 70
Breakfast: Blueberry Almond Pancake
Lunch: Beef & Mushroom Stir-Fry
Dinner: Garlic Rosemary Chicken Drumsticks
Snack: Greek Yogurt Dip with Cucumber Slices

WEEK 11

Day 71
Breakfast: Greek Yogurt & Egg Breakfast Skillet
Lunch: Spicy Chicken & Veggie Lettuce Wraps
Dinner: Spaghetti Squash Marinara with Ground Turkey
Snack: Avocado Toast with Smoked Salmon

Day 72
Breakfast: Sautéed Kale & Turkey Bacon Scramble
Lunch: Garlic Mushroom & Chicken Stir-Fry
Dinner: Rosemary & Honey Glazed Pork Tenderloin
Snack: Caprese Skewers

Day 73
Breakfast: Cottage Cheese & Avocado Toast
Lunch: Greek Chicken & Cauliflower Rice Bowl
Dinner: Lemon Garlic Tilapia with Spinach
Snack: Spicy Hummus with Veggie Sticks

Day 74
Breakfast: Banana Almond Butter Pancakes
Lunch: Herbed Turkey Cutlets with Spinach
Dinner: Baked Lemon Pepper Trout
Snack: Almond Butter & Banana Bites

Day 75
Breakfast: One-Pan Ham & Cheese Breakfast Roll-Up
Lunch: Teriyaki Turkey & Vegetable Stir-Fry
Dinner: Ginger Soy Beef & Bok Choy Stir-Fry
Snack: Greek Yogurt Dip with Cucumber Slices

Day 76
Breakfast: Spicy Egg & Turkey Sausage Skillet
Lunch: Cajun Salmon & Spinach Sauté
Dinner: Seared Lamb Cutlets with Mint Yogurt Sauce
Snack: Energy-Boosting Trail Mix
k Choy Stir-Fry
Snack: Greek Yogurt Dip with Cucumber Slices

Day 77
Breakfast: Coconut Chia Pudding with Berries
Lunch: Honey Mustard Salmon & Zucchini
Dinner: Honey Glazed Pork Belly with Bok Choy
Snack: Stuffed Mini Bell Peppers with Goat Cheese

WEEK 12

Day 78
Breakfast: Savory Egg & Avocado Quesadilla
Lunch: Lemon Garlic Salmon & Asparagus
Dinner: Beef and Vegetable Stew
Snack: Spicy Roasted Chickpeas

Day 79
Breakfast: Smoked Salmon & Spinach Breakfast Wrap
Lunch: Spicy Beef & Broccoli Stir-Fry
Dinner: Garlic Herb Lamb Steaks with Mashed Cauliflower
Snack: Caprese Skewers

Day 80
Breakfast: Cinnamon Ricotta & Honey Toast
Lunch: Quick Lemon Herb Chicken Bowl
Dinner: Lemon Thyme Roast Chicken Thighs
Snack: Avocado Toast with Smoked Salmon

Day 81
Breakfast: Spinach & Feta Egg Skillet
Lunch: Ground Beef & Zucchini Stir-Fry
Dinner: Coconut Curry Shrimp & Spinach
Snack: Energy-Boosting Trail Mix

Day 82
Breakfast: Tomato & Basil Scrambled Eggs
Lunch: Italian Chicken & Tomato Sauté
Dinner: Parmesan-Crusted Pork Chops & Brussels Sprouts
Snack: Almond Butter & Banana Bites

Day 83
Breakfast: Avocado & Smoked Salmon Breakfast Bowl
Lunch: Garlic Shrimp & Spinach Stir-Fry
Dinner: Creamy Coconut Chicken Soup
Snack: Spicy Hummus with Veggie Sticks

Day 84
Breakfast: Sweet Potato & Sausage Hash
Lunch: Lemon Garlic Shrimp & Asparagus
Dinner: Zesty Shrimp & Cauliflower Rice
Snack: Stuffed Mini Bell Peppers with Goat Cheese

WEEK 13

Day 85
Breakfast: Kale & Parmesan Breakfast Scramble
Lunch: Teriyaki Turkey & Vegetable Stir-Fry
Dinner: Balsamic Glazed Chicken & Roasted Carrots
Snack: Spicy Roasted Chickpeas

Day 86
Breakfast: Mushroom & Goat Cheese Omelet
Lunch: Sesame Chicken & Snow Pea Stir-Fry
Dinner: Spiced Lamb Meatballs with Tomato Sauce
Snack: Energy-Boosting Trail Mix

Day 87
Breakfast: Apple Cinnamon Oat Skillet
Lunch: Turkey & Zucchini Skillet
Dinner: Creamy Tomato Basil Soup
Snack: Almond Butter & Banana Bites

Day 88
Breakfast: Zucchini & Cheese Egg Bake
Lunch: Lemon Herb Grilled Chicken Salad
Dinner: Lemon Garlic Cod with Steamed Vegetables
Snack: Avocado Toast with Smoked Salmon

Day 89
Breakfast: Bell Pepper Egg-in-a-Hole
Lunch: Beef & Bell Pepper Fajita Bowl
Dinner: Thai Basil Chicken Stir-Fry
Snack: Greek Yogurt Dip with Cucumber Slices

Day 90
Breakfast: Blueberry Almond Pancake
Lunch: Garlic Butter Shrimp & Zoodles
Dinner: Honey Mustard Pork Chops & Brussels Sprouts
Snack: Stuffed Mini Bell Peppers with Goat Cheese

WEEK 1

Vegetables
Spinach (10 cups)
Cherry tomatoes (2 cups + 10 for skewers)
Bell peppers (5 large + 10 mini)
Zucchini (2 medium)
Sweet potatoes (1 small)
Kale (2 cups)
Mushrooms (¼ cup sliced)
Asparagus (3 cups, trimmed)
Broccoli (1½ cups)
Baby carrots (1 cup)
Mixed vegetables (2 cups)
Cucumber (1, sliced)
Garlic (10 cloves)
Fresh ginger (1 knob, grated)

Fruits
Avocado (4, ripe)
Lemon (8)
Lime (1)
Banana (1)
Apple (½)

Herbs
Fresh basil (2 tbsp, chopped)
Fresh parsley (1 tbsp, chopped)
Fresh rosemary (2 tsp, chopped)
Fresh dill (optional, for garnish)

Meat & Seafood
Chicken:
Boneless, skinless chicken breasts (8)
Bone-in, skin-on chicken thighs (2)
Beef:
Steak (sirloin or ribeye, 1)
Ground beef (1 cup)
Turkey:
Ground turkey (2 cups)
Turkey sausages (4, sliced)

Seafood:
Raw shrimp (3 cups, peeled and deveined)
Salmon fillets (4)

Eggs (14 large)

Dairy
Feta cheese (¾ cup, crumbled)
Parmesan cheese (2 tbsp, grated)
Goat cheese (½ cup, crumbled)

Greek yogurt (1½ cups)

Grains
Quinoa (1 cup, cooked)
Rolled oats (½ cup)
Whole-grain bread (4 slices)
Whole-grain tortilla or wrap (2)

Nuts & Seeds
Almonds (¼ cup)
Walnuts (¼ cup)
Pumpkin seeds (¼ cup)

Legumes
Canned chickpeas (1 can, 15 oz)

Oils & Condiments
Olive oil (14 tbsp)
Butter (2 tbsp)
Dijon mustard (2 tbsp)
Honey (2 tbsp)
Soy sauce (2 tbsp)
Balsamic vinegar (1 tbsp)

Spices
Salt (to taste)
Pepper (to taste)
Red pepper flakes (¼ tsp)
Ground cumin (½ tsp)
Paprika (½ tsp)
Curry powder (1 tbsp)
Cinnamon (¼ tsp)

Miscellaneous
Almond butter (2 tbsp)
Coconut milk (1½ cups)

WEEK 2

Vegetables
Zucchini (3 medium)
Bell peppers (3 large)
Cherry tomatoes (1½ cups)
Snow peas (1 cup)
Brussels sprouts (2 cups, halved)
Spinach (3 cups)
Kale (2 cups, chopped)
Broccoli (1 cup)
Mushrooms (1½ cups, sliced)
Mixed vegetables (2 cups)
Garlic (10 cloves)
Onion (1, diced)

Fruits

Avocado (3, ripe)
Lemon (6)
Banana (1)

Herbs
Fresh basil (1 tbsp, chopped)
Fresh parsley (1 tbsp, chopped)
Fresh thyme (1 tsp)
Fresh dill (optional, for garnish)

Meat & Seafood
Boneless, skinless chicken breasts (5)
Chicken thighs, bone-in, skin-on (2)
Turkey sausages (4, sliced)
Ground turkey (2 cups)
Turkey bacon (2 slices)
Boneless pork chops (2)
Ground beef (1½ cups)
Thinly sliced beef (1½ cups)
Shrimp (3 cups, peeled and deveined)
Salmon fillets (2, 4 oz each)

Eggs (18 large)

Dairy
Parmesan cheese (¼ cup, grated)
Cottage cheese (¼ cup)
Goat cheese (½ cup, crumbled)
Greek yogurt (½ cup)

Grains
Almond flour (½ cup)
Whole-grain bread (3 slices)
Whole-grain tortilla or wrap (1)
Pasta (1 cup, cooked)

Legumes
Canned chickpeas (2 cans, 15 oz)

Nuts & Seeds
Almond butter (3 tbsp)
Oils & Condiments
Olive oil (14 tbsp)
Butter (2 tbsp)
Dijon mustard (1 tbsp)
Soy sauce (2 tbsp)

Spices
Salt (to taste)
Pepper (to taste)
Paprika (½ tsp)
Red pepper flakes (½ tsp)
Cajun seasoning (1 tsp)
Cumin (½ tsp)
Cinnamon (¼ tsp)

Vegetables
Spinach (4 cups, fresh)
Zucchini (3 medium)
Cauliflower rice (1 cup)
Bok choy (2 cups)
Bell peppers (2 large)
Cherry tomatoes (1½ cups, halved)
Steamed vegetables (e.g., broccoli, carrots, 2 cups)
Cucumber (1 large)
Spaghetti squash (1 medium)
Avocado (4, ripe)
Garlic (10 cloves)
Onion (1, diced)

Fruits
Lemon (4)
Lime (1)
Banana (1)
Berries (½ cup mixed)

Herbs
Fresh basil (1 tbsp, chopped)
Fresh parsley (1 tbsp, chopped)
Fresh thyme (1 tsp, chopped)
Fresh dill (optional, for garnish)

Meat & Seafood
Boneless, skinless chicken breasts (5)
Chicken thighs, bone-in, skin-on (4)
Turkey sausages (2)
Ground turkey (1½ cups)
Herbed turkey meatballs (½ lb, ground turkey)
Ground beef (1 cup)
Beef strips (1 cup, thinly sliced)
Cod fillets (2, 4 oz each)
Salmon fillets (2, 4 oz each)
Smoked salmon (4 oz)
Ham slices (1, large)

Eggs (17 large)

Dairy
Feta cheese (¼ cup, crumbled)
Ricotta cheese (¼ cup)
Goat cheese (½ cup, crumbled)
Shredded cheese (½ cup, cheddar or mozzarella)
Greek yogurt (1 cup)

Grains

Whole-grain tortilla or wrap (2 small)
Spaghetti squash (1 medium)
Noodles (2 cups, zucchini noodles)

Legumes
Chickpeas (1 can, 15 oz)

Nuts & Seeds:
Chia seeds (¼ cup)
Almond butter (1 tbsp)
Trail mix ingredients: almonds, walnuts, pumpkin seeds, dried cranberries (¼ cup each)

Oils & Condiments
Olive oil (15 tbsp)
Soy sauce (2 tbsp)
Teriyaki sauce (1 tbsp)
Honey (1 tbsp)
Dijon mustard (1 tbsp)

Spices
Salt (to taste)
Pepper (to taste)
Paprika (½ tsp)
Red pepper flakes (½ tsp)
Italian seasoning (1 tsp)
Cinnamon (½ tsp)

Miscellaneous
Hummus (1 cup)

WEEK 4

Vegetables:
Spinach (6 cups, fresh)
Zucchini (4 medium)
Sweet potato (1 small, diced)
Kale (2 cups, chopped, stems removed)
Broccoli florets (2 cups)
Mushrooms (1¼ cups, sliced)
Bell peppers (4 large, mixed colors)
Cherry tomatoes (¾ cup, halved)
Green beans (1 cup, trimmed)
Lettuce leaves (4 large, for wraps)
Baby carrots (1 cup)
Mini bell peppers (10, halved)

Fruits
Avocado (4)
Apple (1, diced)
Lemon (4)
Banana (1)
Orange (1)

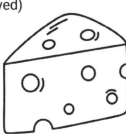

Herbs:
Fresh basil (1 tbsp, chopped)
Fresh rosemary (2 tsp, chopped)
Fresh parsley (1 tbsp, chopped)
Fresh dill (optional, for garnish)

Meat & Seafood
Boneless, skinless chicken breasts (4)
Chicken thighs, bone-in, skin-on (4)
Chicken tenders (1 cup)
Chicken drumsticks (4)
Turkey sausages (2)
Ground turkey (1 cup)
Turkey cutlets (2)
Ground beef (1 cup)
Salmon fillets (3, 4 oz each)
Shrimp (2 cups, raw, peeled and deveined)
Smoked salmon (6 oz)
Duck breast (1)
Breakfast sausage (½ cup, sliced)

Eggs (19 large)
Dairy
Parmesan cheese (4 tbsp, grated)
Goat cheese (½ cup, crumbled)
Greek yogurt (1 cup)

Grains
Whole-grain tortilla or wrap (2 small)
Rolled oats (½ cup)
Zucchini noodles (2 cups)
Legumes
Chickpeas (2 cans, 15 oz each)

Nuts & Seeds
Almond butter (1 tbsp)
Oils & Condiments
Olive oil (16 tbsp)
Balsamic vinegar (1 tbsp)
Honey (2 tbsp)
Dijon mustard (2 tbsp)
Teriyaki sauce (1 tbsp)

Spices
Salt (to taste)
Pepper (to taste)
Red pepper flakes (½ tsp)
Italian seasoning (1 tsp)

Miscellaneous
Hummus (1 cup)

WEEK 5

Vegetables:
Bell peppers (6 large, mixed colors)
Spinach (6 cups, fresh)
Snow peas (1 cup)
Zucchini (2 medium)
Kale (1 cup, chopped)
Brussels sprouts (1 cup, halved)
Broccoli florets (1 cup)
Mushrooms (1 cup, sliced)
Cherry tomatoes (½ cup, halved)
Cucumber (1, sliced)

Fruits:
Blueberries (¼ cup, fresh)
Avocado (3)
Banana (2)
Lemon (4)

Herbs:
Fresh rosemary (2 tsp, chopped)
Fresh mint (1 tbsp, chopped)
Fresh parsley (optional, for garnish)

Meat & Seafood
Boneless, skinless chicken breasts (4)
Turkey bacon (2 slices)
Ground turkey (1 cup)
Ribeye steak (1, 8 oz)
Ground beef (1 cup)
Lamb chops (4 small)
Lamb cutlets (4)
Ground lamb (½ lb)
Pork tenderloin (1, 8 oz)
Boneless pork chops (2)
Shrimp (2 cups, raw, peeled and deveined)
Salmon fillets (2, 4 oz each)
Smoked salmon (4 oz)

Eggs (16 large)

Dairy
Cottage cheese (¼ cup)
Goat cheese (½ cup, crumbled)
Greek yogurt (1½ cups, plain)

Grains
Almond flour (½ cup)
Whole-grain tortilla or wrap (1 small)
Legumes
Chickpeas (1 can, 15 oz)

Nuts & Seeds
Almond butter (2 tbsp)
Energy-boosting trail mix (¼ cup almonds, ¼ cup walnuts, ¼ cup pumpkin seeds, ¼ cup dried cranberries, ¼ cup dark chocolate chips)

Oils & Condiments
Olive oil (14 tbsp)
Dijon mustard (1 tbsp)
Honey (2 tbsp)
Tomato sauce (1 cup)

Spices
Salt (to taste)
Pepper (to taste)
Paprika (½ tsp)
Italian herbs (1 tsp)
Cumin (1 tsp)
Red pepper flakes (optional, for hummus garnish)

Miscellaneous
Hummus (1 cup)

WEEK 6

Vegetables
Bell peppers (3 large, mixed colors)
Spinach (6½ cups, fresh)
Zucchini (2 medium)
Bok choy (1 cup, chopped)
Cauliflower (1 cup, steamed and mashed)
Asparagus (2 cups, trimmed)
Broccoli florets (1 cup)
Mushrooms (1½ cups, sliced)
Cherry tomatoes (1½ cups, halved)
Cucumber (1, sliced)
Mini bell peppers (10, halved and seeds removed)

Fruits
Avocado (4)
Banana (2)
Lemon (4)
Berries (½ cup, mixed)
Herbs
Fresh basil (1 tbsp, chopped)
Fresh parsley (optional, for garnish)
Fresh rosemary (1 tsp, chopped)
Fresh dill (1 tsp, chopped)

Meat & Seafood
Boneless, skinless chicken breasts (4)
Turkey sausage (2 sausages, sliced)

Ground turkey (1 cup)
Beef tenderloin steaks (2, 4 oz each)
Thinly sliced beef (1 cup)
Lamb steaks (2)
Pork belly (½ lb, sliced)
Shrimp (2½ cups, large, peeled and deveined)
Salmon fillets (4, 4 oz each)
Cod fillets (2, 4 oz each)
Smoked salmon (4 oz)

Eggs (16 large)

Dairy

Feta cheese (¼ cup, crumbled)
Goat cheese (½ cup, crumbled)
Ricotta cheese (¼ cup)
Greek yogurt (1½ cups, plain)

Grains:

Tortilla or whole-grain wrap (1 small)
Coconut milk (1½ cups)

Legumes

Chickpeas (1 can, 15 oz)
Nuts & Seeds
Chia seeds (¼ cup)
Almond butter (2 tbsp)
Energy-boosting trail mix (¼ cup almonds, ¼ cup walnuts, ¼ cup pumpkin seeds, ¼ cup dried cranberries, ¼ cup dark chocolate chips)

Oils & Condiments

Olive oil (15 tbsp)
Butter (2 tbsp)
Dijon mustard (1 tbsp)
Honey (3 tbsp)
Balsamic vinegar (1 tbsp)
Soy sauce (2 tbsp)
Teriyaki sauce (1 tbsp)

Spices

Salt (to taste)
Pepper (to taste)
Chili powder (½ tsp)
Paprika (optional, for garnish)

Miscellaneous

Hummus (1 cup)

Vegetables

Spinach (6 cups)
Zucchini (2, medium)
Sweet potato (1 small)
Kale (1 cup, chopped)
Mushrooms (1¼ cups, sliced)
Broccoli florets (2 cups)
Brussels sprouts (1 cup, halved)
Bell peppers (4 large, mixed colors)
Cherry tomatoes (10, for Caprese Skewers)
Cucumber (1, sliced)
Mini bell peppers (10, halved and seeds removed)

Fruits

Avocado (4)
Banana (2)
Lemon (5)
Apple (½, diced)

Herbs

Fresh basil (1 tbsp, chopped + 10 leaves for Caprese Skewers)
Fresh parsley (optional, for garnish)
Fresh dill (1 tsp, chopped)
Fresh thyme (1 tsp, chopped)

Meat & Seafood

Boneless, skinless chicken breasts (4)
Turkey sausage (2 sausages, sliced)
Ground turkey (1 cup)
Ground beef (1 cup)
Thinly sliced beef (1 cup)
Boneless pork chops (2)
Salmon fillets (4, 4 oz each)
Tuna steaks (2, 4 oz each)
Tilapia fillets (2)
Trout fillets (2)
Shrimp (1½ cups, peeled and deveined)
Smoked salmon (4 oz)

Eggs (16 large)

Dairy

Goat cheese (½ cup, crumbled)
Parmesan cheese (4 tbsp, grated)
Greek yogurt (1 cup)
Mozzarella balls (10, fresh, small)

Grains

Oats (½ cup, rolled)
Zucchini noodles (zoodles) (2 cups)

Legumes
Chickpeas (1 can, 15 oz)

Nuts & Seeds
Almond butter (2 tbsp)
Energy-boosting trail mix (¼ cup almonds, ¼ cup walnuts, ¼ cup pumpkin seeds, ¼ cup dried cranberries, ¼ cup dark chocolate chips)

Oils & Condiments
Olive oil (16 tbsp)
Butter (1 tbsp)
Dijon mustard (1 tbsp)
Soy sauce (1 tbsp)
Hummus (1 cup)

Spices
Salt (to taste)
Pepper (to taste)
Garlic powder (optional, for seasoning)
Paprika (optional, for garnish)

Miscellaneous
Balsamic glaze (for Caprese Skewers)

WEEK 8

Vegetables
Spinach (7 cups)
Zucchini (2, medium)
Kale (2 cups, chopped)
Mushrooms (1¼ cups, sliced)
Bell peppers (7, mixed colors)
Sweet potato (1 small, diced)
Broccoli florets (1 cup)
Mini bell peppers (10, halved and seeds removed)
Cauliflower rice (1½ cups)
Cherry tomatoes (1½ cups, halved)
Cucumber (1, sliced)
Baby carrots (1 cup)
Mixed vegetables (e.g., carrots, broccoli, zucchini, 1 cup)

Fruits
Banana (3, ripe)
Avocado (5)
Lemon (7)
Lime (1)
Blueberries (¼ cup, fresh)

Herbs
Fresh basil (1 tbsp, chopped + 10 leaves for Caprese Skewers)

Fresh parsley (optional, for garnish)
Fresh rosemary (2 tsp, chopped)
Fresh thyme (1 tsp, chopped)

Meat & Seafood
Boneless, skinless chicken breasts (4)
Chicken thighs (6)
Turkey bacon (2 slices, chopped)
Ground turkey (1½ cups)
Thinly sliced beef (1½ cups)
Steak (such as sirloin or ribeye, 8 oz, sliced into strips)
Boneless pork chops (2)
Shrimp (2½ cups, peeled and deveined)
Smoked salmon (4 oz)
Salmon fillets (2, 4 oz each)

Eggs (19 large)

Dairy
Goat cheese (½ cup, crumbled)
Parmesan cheese (3 tbsp, grated)
Cottage cheese (¼ cup)
Greek yogurt (1½ cups)
Mozzarella balls (10, fresh, small)

Grains
Almond flour (½ cup)
Spaghetti squash (1 cup, cooked)
Oats (½ cup, rolled)

Nuts & Seeds
Almond butter (3 tbsp)
Energy-boosting trail mix (¼ cup almonds, ¼ cup walnuts, ¼ cup pumpkin seeds, ¼ cup dried cranberries, ¼ cup dark chocolate chips)

Oils & Condiments
Olive oil (18 tbsp)
Butter (1 tbsp)
Dijon mustard (1 tbsp)
Soy sauce (2 tbsp)
Hummus (1 cup)

Spices
Salt (to taste)
Pepper (to taste)
Garlic powder (optional, for seasoning)
Paprika (optional, for garnish)

Miscellaneous
Balsamic glaze (for Caprese Skewers)
Coconut milk (½ cup, for curry)
Curry powder (1 tbsp)

WEEK 9

Vegetables
Spinach (9 cups, fresh)
Zucchini (2 medium)
Bell peppers (10, mixed colors)
Broccoli florets (3 cups)
Cauliflower rice (1 cup)
Cherry tomatoes (1½ cups, halved)
Mini bell peppers (10, halved and seeds removed)
Asparagus (1 cup, trimmed)
Baby carrots (optional, for snack platter)
Mixed vegetables (e.g., carrots, broccoli, zucchini, 1 cup)

Fruits
Banana (2, ripe)
Avocado (4)
Lemon (6)
Lime (1)
Berries (½ cup, mixed)

Herbs
Fresh basil (1 tbsp, chopped)
Fresh parsley (optional, for garnish)
Fresh mint (1 tbsp, chopped)
Fresh rosemary (1 tsp, chopped)
Fresh thyme (1 tsp, chopped)

Meat & Seafood
Boneless, skinless chicken breasts (5)
Ground turkey (1 cup)
Ground chicken (optional, for Italian sauté)
Thinly sliced beef (1½ cups)
Ground beef (1 cup)
Beef tenderloin steaks (2, 4 oz each)
Lamb meatballs (ingredients listed below)
Lamb cutlets (4, small)
Salmon fillets (2, 4 oz each)
Cod fillets (2, 4 oz each)
Shrimp (2 cups, peeled and deveined)
Smoked salmon (4 oz)
Duck breast (1, 4 oz)

Eggs (20 large)

Dairy
Goat cheese (½ cup, crumbled)
Parmesan cheese (2 tbsp, grated)
Ricotta cheese (¼ cup)
Greek yogurt (1½ cups)
Mozzarella balls (10, fresh, small)

Grains
Almond flour (optional, for thickening sauces)
Spaghetti squash (1 cup, cooked)

Nuts & Seeds
Almond butter (3 tbsp)
Chia seeds (¼ cup)
Energy-boosting trail mix (¼ cup almonds, ¼ cup walnuts, ¼ cup pumpkin seeds, ¼ cup dried cranberries, ¼ cup dark chocolate chips)

Oils & Condiments
Olive oil (20 tbsp)
Butter (2 tbsp)
Dijon mustard (1 tbsp)
Soy sauce (2 tbsp)
Balsamic vinegar (1 tbsp)
Honey (optional, for drizzling)

Spices
Salt (to taste)
Pepper (to taste)
Garlic powder (optional, for seasoning)
Paprika (optional, for garnish)
Curry powder (1 tbsp)

Miscellaneous
Hummus (1 cup)
Coconut milk (½ cup, for curry)
Tomato sauce (1 cup)

WEEK 10

Vegetables
Sweet potatoes (2 small, diced)
Kale (3 cups, chopped)
Zucchini (3 medium, diced)
Bell peppers (6, mixed colors, sliced)
Broccoli florets (optional, for stir-fry, 1 cup)
Cherry tomatoes (½ cup, halved)
Mushrooms (1½ cups, sliced)
Mini bell peppers (10, halved)
Spinach (2 cups, fresh)
Asparagus (2 cups, trimmed)
Green beans (1 cup, trimmed)
Baby carrots (optional, for stew, ½ cup)
Mixed vegetables (e.g., carrots, broccoli, zucchini, 1 cup for steaming)

Fruits
Banana (3, ripe)

Blueberries (½ cup, fresh)
Apple (1, diced)
Lemon (5)
Lime (1)

Herbs
Fresh parsley (optional, for garnish)
Fresh basil (1 tbsp, chopped)
Fresh thyme (1 tsp, chopped)
Fresh rosemary (2 tsp, chopped)

Meat & Seafood
Boneless, skinless chicken breasts (4)
Chicken drumsticks (4)
Ground turkey (2 cups)
Ground beef (1 cup)
Thinly sliced beef (1 cup)
Lamb chops (4, small)
Cod fillets (2, 4 oz each)
Salmon fillets (2, 4 oz each)
Halibut fillets (2, 4 oz each)
Shrimp (2 cups, peeled and deveined)
Smoked salmon (4 oz)

Eggs (18 large)

Dairy
Goat cheese (½ cup, crumbled)
Parmesan cheese (2 tbsp, grated)
Greek yogurt (1 cup)
Mozzarella balls (10, fresh, small)

Grains
Almond flour (optional, for pancakes)
Spaghetti squash (1 cup, cooked)
Rolled oats (½ cup)

Nuts & Seeds
Almond butter (2 tbsp)
Energy-boosting trail mix (¼ cup almonds, ¼ cup walnuts, ¼ cup pumpkin seeds, ¼ cup dried cranberries, ¼ cup dark chocolate chips)

Oils & Condiments
Olive oil (18 tbsp)
Butter (2 tbsp)
Dijon mustard (1 tbsp)
Soy sauce (1 tbsp)
Honey (optional, for chicken)

Spices
Salt (to taste)
Pepper (to taste)
Garlic powder (optional, for seasoning)

Paprika (optional, for garnish)
Miscellaneous
Hummus (1 cup)
Tomato sauce (1 cup)
Coconut milk (½ cup, for curry)

WEEK 11

Vegetables
Kale (3 cups, chopped)
Spinach (6 cups, fresh)
Zucchini (3 medium, sliced)
Bok choy (2 cups, chopped)
Bell peppers (3, diced)
Mushrooms (1½ cups, sliced)
Cauliflower rice (1 cup)
Cherry tomatoes (1½ cups, halved)
Cucumber (1, sliced)
Mini bell peppers (10, halved)
Lettuce leaves (4 large)
Spaghetti squash (1 cup, cooked)
Avocado (4, ripe)
Bananas (3, ripe)
Lemon (6)
Lime (optional, for trail mix, 1)

Herbs
Fresh basil (2 tbsp, chopped)
Fresh parsley (optional, for garnish)
Fresh mint (2 tbsp, chopped)
Fresh rosemary (2 tsp, chopped)

Meat & Seafood
Boneless, skinless chicken breasts (6)
Turkey bacon (2 slices)
Ground turkey (2 cups)
Turkey sausage (2)
Turkey cutlets (2)
Thinly sliced beef (1 cup)
Pork tenderloin (8 oz)
Pork belly (8 oz, sliced)
Lamb cutlets (4)
Tilapia fillets (2, 4 oz each)
Salmon fillets (4, 4 oz each)
Smoked salmon (4 oz)
Trout fillets (2, 4 oz each)

Eggs (18 large)
Dairy
Cottage cheese (½ cup)
Goat cheese (½ cup, crumbled)
Parmesan cheese (2 tbsp, grated)

Greek yogurt (1½ cups)
Shredded cheese (cheddar or mozzarella, ¼ cup)
Fresh mozzarella balls (10, small)

Grains
Rolled oats (½ cup, for pancakes)
Almond flour (optional, for pancakes)

Nuts & Seeds
Almond butter (3 tbsp)
Chia seeds (¼ cup, for pudding)
Energy-boosting trail mix (¼ cup almonds, ¼ cup walnuts, ¼ cup pumpkin seeds, ¼ cup dried cranberries, ¼ cup dark chocolate chips)

Oils & Condiments
Olive oil (18 tbsp)
Butter (2 tbsp)
Dijon mustard (optional, 1 tbsp)
Honey (2 tbsp, for glazing pork and pork belly)
Balsamic vinegar (1 tbsp, optional for flavor)

Spices
Salt (to taste)
Pepper (to taste)
Garlic powder (optional, for seasoning)
Red pepper flakes (optional, for spiciness)
Miscellaneous
Hummus (1 cup)
Tomato sauce (1 cup)
Soy sauce (1 tbsp)
Coconut milk (optional, ½ cup)

WEEK 12

Vegetables
Spinach (8 cups, fresh)
Zucchini (3 medium)
Broccoli (2 cups, florets)
Cauliflower (1 cup, mashed)
Cherry tomatoes (2½ cups, halved)
Asparagus (4 cups, trimmed)
Sweet potatoes (1 small, diced)
Bell peppers (2, diced)
Mini bell peppers (10, halved)
Mushrooms (1 cup, sliced)
Brussels sprouts (1 cup, halved)
Onion (2, diced)
Carrots (½ cup, diced)
Potatoes (½ cup, diced)

Kale (optional, 1 cup, chopped)

Herbs
Fresh basil (2 tbsp, chopped)
Fresh parsley (1 tbsp, chopped)
Fresh thyme (1 tsp, chopped)
Fresh rosemary (1 tsp, chopped)

Fruits
Bananas (3, ripe)
Avocados (5, ripe)
Lemon (7)

Meat & Seafood
Boneless, skinless chicken breasts (4)
Chicken thighs (2, bone-in, skin-on)
Ground chicken (1 cup)
Ground beef (3 cups)
Beef (stewing cubes, 1 cup)
Thinly sliced beef (1 cup)
Pork chops (2, boneless)
Lamb steaks (2)
Salmon fillets (4, 4 oz each)
Smoked salmon (4 oz)
Shrimp (3 cups, peeled and deveined)

Eggs (16 large)

Dairy
Ricotta cheese (¼ cup)
Feta cheese (¼ cup, crumbled)
Parmesan cheese (2 tbsp, grated)
Fresh mozzarella balls (10)

Grains
Cauliflower rice (1 cup)
Rolled oats (½ cup)
Tortillas (3 small whole-grain)

Nuts & Seeds
Almond butter (2 tbsp)
Energy-boosting trail mix (¼ cup almonds, ¼ cup walnuts, ¼ cup pumpkin seeds, ¼ cup dried cranberries, ¼ cup dark chocolate chips)

Oils & Condiments:
Olive oil (16 tbsp)
Butter (2 tbsp)
Dijon mustard (1 tbsp)
Coconut milk (1½ cups)

Spices
Salt (to taste)
Pepper (to taste)
Garlic powder (optional, for seasoning)

Curry powder (1 tbsp)
Red pepper flakes (optional, for spiciness)

Miscellaneous
Hummus (1 cup)
Chickpeas (1 can, rinsed and drained)
Soy sauce (1 tbsp)

WEEK 13

Vegetables
Kale (2 cups, chopped)
Zucchini (3 medium)
Bell peppers (4, mixed colors, sliced)
Carrots (1 cup, baby or sliced)
Snow peas (1 cup)
Mushrooms (1¼ cups, sliced)
Spinach (2 cups, fresh)
Cherry tomatoes (1½ cups, halved)
Cucumber (1 large, sliced)
Mixed vegetables (1 cup, e.g., carrots, broccoli)
Brussels sprouts (1 cup, halved)
Onion (2, diced)

Fruits
Apples (1, diced)
Blueberries (¼ cup, fresh)
Bananas (3, ripe)
Avocados (5, ripe)
Lemon (6)

Herbs
Fresh basil (1 tbsp, chopped)
Fresh parsley (1 tbsp, chopped)
Fresh thyme (1 tsp, chopped)
Fresh rosemary (1 tsp, chopped)

Meat & Seafood
Ground turkey (2 cups)
Boneless, skinless chicken breasts (6)
Chicken thighs (2)
Ground beef (1 cup)
Beef strips (1 cup)
Ground lamb (½ lb)
Cod fillets (2, 4 oz each)
Shrimp (1 cup, peeled and deveined)
Smoked salmon (4 oz)

Eggs (20 large)

Dairy
Goat cheese (1 tbsp, crumbled)
Parmesan cheese (2 tbsp, grated)

Greek yogurt (1 cup, plain)

Grains
Rolled oats (½ cup)
Almond flour (½ cup)
Zoodles (2 cups, zucchini noodles)

Nuts & Seeds
Almond butter (2 tbsp)
Energy-boosting trail mix (¼ cup almonds, ¼ cup walnuts, ¼ cup pumpkin seeds, ¼ cup dried cranberries, ¼ cup dark chocolate chips)

Legumes
Chickpeas (1 can, rinsed and drained)

Oils & Condiments
Olive oil (16 tbsp)
Butter (2 tbsp)
Dijon mustard (1 tbsp)
Balsamic vinegar (1 tbsp)

Spices
Salt (to taste)
Pepper (to taste)
Garlic powder (optional, for seasoning)
Cinnamon (¼ tsp)

Miscellaneous
Hummus (½ cup)
Tomato sauce (1 cup)

CONCLUSION

As you reach the final page of The Good Energy Cookbook, you've not only gained a collection of recipes but also a renewed approach to energy, balance, and well-being. This book was crafted to be more than just a guide—it's a companion on your journey toward vibrant health and vitality.

Throughout these pages, you've learned how intentional choices—whether it's what you eat, how you prepare meals, or how you structure your day—can transform how you feel. The nutrient-dense recipes, daily rituals, and mindfulness practices in this book are tools to help you thrive. Each small, consistent step is an investment in your energy, your health, and your happiness.

The recipes here are designed to bring joy to your meals and ease to your routine. They're crafted to work with your body, fueling it with the nourishment it deserves while making healthy living approachable and enjoyable. Alongside them, the principles of mindful eating, wellness journaling, and energy activation create a holistic approach to feeling your best every day.

This journey doesn't end here. These tools and ideas are meant to grow with you. As you revisit the recipes or create your own variations, you'll continue to refine what works best for you. Your experience is unique, and every small change you embrace helps build the vibrant, energetic life you deserve.

If this book has made a difference in your life—whether through a recipe you love, a tip that inspired you, or a new way of thinking about food and energy—your voice matters. Sharing your thoughts with a review on Amazon helps others discover this book and begin their own journey toward good energy. Reviews aren't just helpful; they're the ultimate way to connect with others who are searching for exactly what you've found here.

Thank you for allowing this book to be a part of your journey. May it inspire you to continue exploring, savoring, and thriving—one delicious bite and mindful moment at a time. Here's to living a life full of good energy!

Made in the USA
Middletown, DE
21 March 2025

73073202R00061